Why Wait to Be Great?

WHY
WAIT TO BE
GREAT?

It's Either Now *or* Too Late

TERRY HAWKINS

BK

Berrett–Koehler Publishers, Inc.
San Francisco
a BK Life book

Berrett-Koehler Publishers, Inc.
235 Montgomery Street, Suite 650, San Francisco, CA 94104-2916
Tel: (415) 288-0260 • Fax: (415) 362-2512 • www.bkconnection.com

ORDERING INFORMATION

QUANTITY SALES. Special discounts are available on quantity purchases by corporations, associations, and others. For details, contact the "Special Sales Department" at the Berrett-Koehler address above.

INDIVIDUAL SALES. Berrett-Koehler publications are available through most bookstores. They can also be ordered directly from Berrett-Koehler: Tel: (800) 929-2929; Fax: (802) 864-7626; www.bkconnection.com

ORDERS FOR COLLEGE TEXTBOOK/COURSE ADOPTION USE. Please contact Berrett-Koehler: Tel: (800) 929-2929; Fax: (802) 864-7626.

ORDERS BY U.S. TRADE BOOKSTORES AND WHOLESALERS. Please contact Ingram Publisher Services, Tel: (800) 509-4887; Fax: (800) 838-1149; E-mail: customer.service@ingrampublisherservices.com; or visit www.ingrampublisherservices.com/Ordering for details about electronic ordering.

Berrett-Koehler and the BK logo are registered trademarks of Berrett-Koehler Publishers, Inc.

Printed in the United States of America

Berrett-Koehler books are printed on long-lasting acid-free paper. When it is available, we choose paper that has been manufactured by environmentally responsible processes. These may include using trees grown in sustainable forests, incorporating recycled paper, minimizing chlorine in bleaching, or recycling the energy produced at the paper mill.

LIBRARY OF CONGRESS CATALOGING-IN-PUBLICATION DATA
Hawkins, Terry.
Why wait to be great? : it's either now or too late / Terry Hawkins. —
First Edition.
    pages cm
ISBN 978-1-60994-891-7 (pbk.)
1. Self-actualization (Psychology) 2. Happiness. I. Title.
BF637.S4.H395 2013
158—dc23

                                                                2013005544

FIRST EDITION

17 16 15 14 13   10 9 8 7 6 5 4 3 2 1

Cover design by Irene Morris Design. Project management and interior design by VJBScribe. Copyediting by Kristi Hein. Proofreading by Don Roberts. Index by George Draffan. Illustrations by Mick Tate.

To Lynn

*I thank her for touching my life in ways
that are beyond expression.*

*May the magic of her soul be sprinkled
throughout all of our lives.*

Contents

Preface

I remember telling a few stories from my childhood to a new friend, and she commented that by looking at my website and the success I have had as a businesswoman, speaker, and author, you would think I had led a charmed life. But looks can be deceiving. After thirty years of presenting to thousands and thousands of audiences around the globe, there is one thing I know for sure. We all have a past—events and circumstances that either propel us or keep us trapped in the memory of our pain.

I recall thinking as I was growing up that I was jinxed. Sexual abuse at four, then again from ages five to nine by my music teacher; poverty; being severely pigeon-toed; a disfiguring skin virus from ages five to seventeen; savage beatings; the death of my father and becoming caregiver for my siblings; depression at sixteen, eating disorders, and drinking issues in my late teens; attempted suicide; sexual harassment in my early career—I couldn't understand how life could be so cruel as to give me far more than I thought was my fair share of life's challenges. I fought against the pain in my heart and the confusion in my head for many years. I defined myself by these events and felt worthless for most of my early life—resulting in an abysmal self-esteem and self-image. But I knew how to work hard, and I simply loved helping people.

In my early twenties, the fortune of my career landed me a position with a Japanese/American training organization, and thus began my journey of wanting to know why I felt the way I did, and why I would seemingly, unknowingly, sabotage my own success along the way. The greatest healing I have had in life has come through my relationship with my two beautiful sons, Harison and Jackson, and through the work that I do. (I know, what a cruel mother to spell Harison with one R!) Through these amazing mediums I have been able to use the mirror of my life to finally accept who I really am.

I also realized — through hearing countless stories of other people's shocking tragedies and challenges — that by comparison my life was not that bad at all. In fact, when I saw how some of these people just got on with their lives and used their pain as a passage to their own evolution, it stirred a curiosity in me to discover how we could all become more successful in our lives *because* of our past, not in spite of it. I realized that avoiding our pain turns it to poison, whereas accepting and moving through our pain turns it to fuel and passion.

I became a passionate explorer for understanding where irrational thoughts and behaviors came from and for how I could rewrite my life's script so that my todays and tomorrows were not soaked in the pain of my yesterdays.

I spent many years on the elusive path of finding permanent happiness. I realized after countless disappointments that happiness is not and should not be a goal. It is simply a feeling and, like all feelings, is as transient as the rain. However, the one feeling that can affect me, and all of us, in a negative way is pain. Pain is going to accompany us all throughout our lives — not as a constant companion but as a regular visitor all the same. My years of working with people showed me that we don't need help in dealing with the joyous, happy, calm, peaceful, tranquil moments in our life. It is the tough days; the days when our heart feels heavy and we feel alone. The days when we feel love has passed us by, the days when we want to crawl into a hole and stay there, the days when our unexpressed rage bubbles under the surface—these are the times when we need help.

It is also, however, a journey that must be taken alone. The moment we realize that no one else can walk our path and heal our hurts, regardless of how close we feel to them, is the moment we start owning our life. Others can certainly encourage us, comfort us, and lend a supportive ear to our woes, but in the end it is we, and only we, who can walk into the pain of our past and find the hidden treasures of wisdom, kindness, forgiveness, and acceptance.

My intention for this book is to give you a support system, a process that will guide you through when the path feels too long or you feel all alone. I want to offer you simple yet powerfully effective formulas that you can recall and use with ease to help navigate your way through life.

Now I look at my life as a great mystery and myself as the explorer, and I invite you to do so as well. It's an exciting journey—one that can offer us endless opportunities every day to bring us closer to our hearts and souls. I no longer see the events and pain of my past, present, or future as negatives. I am filled with deep gratitude and humility that I have had and will continue to have the opportunity to experience so many facets of this wonderful life.

When we relinquish our resistance to our pain and realize that it is simply a clue in the mystery of our life, we start to comprehend that the greatest gifts we have are those that we give ourselves internally, not externally.

Enjoy your exploration!

Terry
xx o x

Until one is committed, there is hesitancy, the chance to draw back, always ineffectiveness. Concerning all acts of initiative (and creation), there is one elementary truth, the ignorance of which kills countless ideas and splendid plans: that the moment one definitely commits oneself, Providence moves too. All sorts of things occur to help one that would never otherwise have occurred. A whole stream of events issues from the decision, raising in one's favor all manner of unforeseen incidents, meetings, and material assistance, which no man could have dreamt would have come his way. I learned a deep respect for one of Goethe's couplets:

Whatever you can do or dream you can, begin it.
Boldness has genius, power, and magic in it.

—W. H. MURRAY, *THE SCOTTISH*
HIMALAYAN EXPEDITION

BEGIN IT NOW!

Chapter 1

There Are Only Two Times in Life: Now and Too Late!

We all have a story. The basic premise of living provides us with a smorgasbord of possible opportunities to add to our story. We gather stories within our story, and the longer we live, the more "scenes" we add; thus by the end of our life we have built a story that is long, rich, and completely unique to us. No one else ever has or ever will have *our* story—this is one of the most amazing miracles of life.

As much as our stories may differ, they also unite us in one common element that no human being can ever avoid—our ability to feel. Our stories trigger a variety of feelings that can either propel us forward or keep us stifled and paralyzed in the past.

We often hear people say that it is the events and experiences of our lives that shape us into who we are, but is that really the case? Why is it that two people can experience the same event and yet each be affected in a completely different way? Is it the story of our life that determines our happiness, or is it the position from which we view our story—the story we tell ourselves about our story? Is it this interpretation that affects the decisions we make, how we feel about our life, and how we feel about those in it?

Many years ago I was sitting in my office, reading through the participant list for the next management training program I was conducting for one of our clients. While scrolling, I noticed a handwritten note beside one of the names. It read: *Lynn—husband died four weeks ago.* Lynn had participated in our sales and service program just over a year earlier.

When the course began, we started introducing ourselves to one another. Eventually, it was Lynn's turn to speak. When I asked her how she was feeling, she replied, "Not that good!" Not recalling that note, I thoughtlessly said, "Oh, why not? It can't be that bad!" Her face reddened and her eyes filled with tears, and in that moment I remembered the note. *She* was the one whose husband who had died four weeks earlier. I didn't know what to say. I couldn't imagine what it was like to experience that kind of loss. I felt so stupid and awkward for being flippant. Yet despite my obvious discomfort at my faux pas, she responded with warmth and love. She said that she had come to the program because she wanted to laugh again, as her recent life had been so sad, and she was happy to be here.

That night, when I went to bed in my hotel room, I decided to let my imagination run wild, without boundaries. I tried to imagine what it would be like to lose someone that close to me—someone I loved with all my heart. I imagined myself never having that person in my life again. I fully associated with the thought. It hurt. The pain spread through every limb, every vein, and every heartbeat. It was almost too much for me to bear. Yet in the training room I had seen a woman with the courage to confront her deepest anguish and face the world, allowing herself to laugh and cry as she needed to.

Lynn spent the next couple of days immersing herself in the program. During one particular section she actually laughed so much she cried. As she wiped away the tears, she told us how wonderful it was to be crying from happiness, not sadness. It's hard to find the words to describe the special feeling of watching someone experience joy again after so much sadness. When Lynn talked about her husband, her entire face lit up. He was her soul mate, her lover, her everything! Before meeting him, she had spent many years in an unhappy marriage. This wonderful man had finally given her the joy that had eluded her with her first husband.

Lynn told us that they had been building their dream home, and to speed things along financially, he had moved from his position at the Customs Department (where he had worked for twenty years) to take up a position as a courier. Six weeks later, he had walked into a building and unknowingly inhaled the deadly bacteria for Legionnaires' disease. Ten days later, he was dead. Her mate, her lover, her confidant, her friend, was gone.

I looked at the sadness in her eyes and felt an urgent need to take her emptiness away. I desperately wanted her to be happy, and I realized that I was responding to my own fears of losing those that I loved. Grief is a necessary part of healing. By wanting Lynn to not feel her grief, I was trying to protect myself from the pain of death. We try so hard to run away from the really painful emotions of life, yet they must be experienced; otherwise, we can't move on.

Over the next twelve months, I saw Lynn a few times at my presentations and workshops. We also sent each other occasional e-mails, including one about a monkey that made her laugh so much she got a stitch in her side! In one of those e-mails, she asked me to make a voice recording for her. She said she needed something from me that spoke to her—and her alone—to get her through the dark days.

She said, "Terry, you say things that inspire me and make me feel alive. Get me out of this rut I'm in. Make me a recording that I can play in the car when I'm feeling down."

I promised her I would send it.

The next time I saw Lynn was a few months later at a one-day workshop I was conducting. She asked about the recording, and I apologized for not sending it. I confessed that I was so nervous about what she might think that I hadn't gotten around to doing it; I didn't want to embarrass myself. She reassured me, encouraged me, and even begged me to do it. We had a few laughs and a big hug, and I promised her I would do it by Christmas.

Well, time rolled by, and I thought about that recording nearly every day. I kept thinking about how special Lynn was and how pathetic I was for procrastinating. But in truth, I was nervous about what others might think of what I would say. I kept asking myself what I was waiting for. Did I need my message to be perfect? Should it be profound? And who was I to judge that anyway?

I was paralyzed with indecision just thinking about it! Then came the new year, and the phone rang.

"Do you know Lynn from Perth?"

"Why, yes!" I said with a touch of guilt, remembering the unfinished recording.

"She died last night in her sleep."

✳

There are only two times in life: NOW and TOO LATE!

I state that phrase nearly every day of my life. For the most part, I live it, because there really are only two times in life — this moment, and then it's gone! If this is the case, then why do so many of us wait to be great? Why do we get so stymied by life that we become frozen? Why does it become so difficult to seize each moment with passion and courage? Is it because we are afraid?

We all get afraid at times, but it's sad when that fear paralyzes us and prevents us from moving forward. This is not a message about physical death. It's a message about the death we have while we're still alive.

That night, I cried for Lynn, and I cried for me. I cried that I hadn't done what she thought I was capable of doing. I cried for the fact that I could have made her life a little easier — but I hadn't. Why?

Because I was afraid!

Life is full of learning experiences for all of us; no one escapes. It's packed with situations that give us wisdom and understanding — but what if those experiences are so painful that we get stuck in the pain and thus stop moving forward?

Not more than twenty-four hours had passed when I received another phone call. It was a second blow. A young man I had worked with a few weeks before—a beautiful, talented, intelligent twenty-one-year-old—had been sentenced to prison for a drug offense. Again there was sadness in my heart. I remembered the beautiful, innocent face of this young man with such a promising future. It was hard to think of him being locked away with hardened criminals in a prison cell, all because of a few unwise choices.

A third blow came a few days later. A friend called to tell me that his eighteen-year-old sister had tried to kill herself. She had jumped off a bridge four floors high—and survived! How desperate must she have been to not see a way out and to make an attempt on her own life?

I wanted to scream and yell for all three of them!

In the course of training and presenting to thousands of audiences, I've heard endless stories about people who have been to hell and back. I've also discovered some lessons and drawn some conclusions from these tragedies and triumphs. The biggest conclusion I've come to is this: I have yet to meet anyone who has had a charmed life. Every one of us has experienced something in our life from which we still carry scars. Some of the scars are self-inflicted, and some are a result of what others have done to us. They vary in intensity, and some are more painful than others. But behind every face lies an amazing story! All of us have been touched by life in some way, and I am reminded of this every day. Whenever I look at a stranger's face, I wonder what story this person could tell me and what painful past lies inside.

Our most painful memories are usually only exacerbated when we try to numb the feeling by running away. I spent many years of my life filled with shame and anger about my past, trying to pretend that it never happened. I too have experienced dark times in which I simply wanted to be able to erase some of those unpleasant, painful memories, and I also spent many of my younger years stuck in that empty hole called "What if?"

A woman so heartbroken, wondering why fate had dealt her such a harsh card; a young man with his whole future in front of him, now facing the stark reality of time in prison; a teenager so desperate to silence her pain, now confronting her own survival. These three — Lynn, the young drug user, and my friend's sister — all had something in common, just as you and I probably do.

What controls their destinies? How will these experiences affect their lives? And is the actual experience the defining moment in their lives?

No!

It is never the actual experience that defines us. It is how we *perceive* these experiences that defines how we will live the rest of our lives. *That* is the defining moment!

All we have is *now*. In each moment we are given the choice of how to interpret and react to each situation. Unfortunately, many of us are completely unaware that we hold the key to our own happiness — we hold the pen that can write the new story of how our life can be.

So let's look at some of the things that get in the way of this happiness and why we wait to be great.

Chapter 2

Get Out of That Pit!

As human beings, it is innate for us to want to improve ourselves and strive for a better life, and I'm sure we've all had those bursts of desire to look after ourselves, to do better. Have you ever been in the mind-set, for example, in which you decided to get fit? You know the feeling—you feel like it's time to turn your life around, to go from being a lazy loafer to a lean, mean, healthy machine.

You start the week like the reincarnation of Olympian Jesse Owens. You set the alarm for 5:30 a.m. The moment it goes off, you spring out of bed and change into your exercise clothes. Off you go, with a bounce in your step and a vision of being the next marathon winner at the Olympic Games. You get on the treadmill and push up that hill. You hop on the weight machines and complete three sets on each. The sweat is dripping from you like Niagara Falls. Ahhh, what a workout!

Day Two. (It's probably safe to say it's a Tuesday.) *Beep! Beep! Beep!* The alarm goes off. This time, you have a little conversation with yourself:

"Gosh, I feel really tired this morning, and I've got a huge day at work ahead of me. My legs are so sore from yesterday's workout. I really think I should take it easy. I could do some serious harm if I overdo it. Maybe I'll sleep in this morning and go to the gym after work. My muscles won't be as sore by then. Yeah! I'll sleep in. I deserve it!"

You hit the snooze button.

Have you ever been in this headspace? We usually go there when we want to implement change in our life—whether it's exercise, eating, communicating differently, completing assignments or work projects, or even vowing to be more patient with our kids. It's that crucial moment when we decide to take a certain path.

So what's the key difference between staying in bed and getting up to go for that run? The answer for me is *Flipman or Pitman?*

In everything we do, we have two possible paths of thinking. One enhances our now, and the other causes us missed opportunities (too late). I have turned these two mind-sets into two characters with whom we can easily identify. The superhero (Flipman) creates and enhances our being. The villain (Pitman) represents the destructive, negative state in which we can exist. I wanted us to have this simple metaphor so we could call ourselves on our own game playing—a metaphor that would make it easy to identify any feelings, thoughts, or behaviors that did not help us move through our pain and out the other side. I wanted us to be able to *choose* our response to life's events in a simple but powerful way, and to stop avoiding the brilliant yet sometimes excruciatingly painful path of self-discovery.

Flipman and Pitman are the lead characters in the internal movie that we play every day inside the movie theater of our mind. This movie enacts our moment-by-moment perceptions of events and situations that occur in our day-to-day life. The plot of this internal movie is the story of our life as it unfolds. With every decision and choice we make, we train our brain to support us in either a Pitman way of life or a Flipman way of life.

When we choose to live in the moment, the *now*, and embrace each experience and what it has to give us, we don't wait to be great. We move forward and evolve—this is Flipman.

When we avoid our pain, whatever that is—the discomfort, the fear, the anxiety of "what if" or "if only," the sadness, the anger, the grief, the frustration, the jealousy, the resentment—we put our life on pause, and Pitman becomes our constant companion. We continue to create results that we don't want and then complain that someone or something did it to us.

Rather than making this another philosophical way to live, I wanted us to have a strategy, a process that we could implement whenever we wanted to choose a more empowered way to live—I wanted us to be able to choose Flipman's Strategy and not Pitman's Path. When we wait to be great, we miss the moment; it's gone, and it's too late. By also understanding Pitman's Path, we can easily identify what stops us from taking action, *now*. In order for us to disempower Pitman, we need a full comprehension of the grasp he can have on our life. Chapters 2 through 9 explore when we are in danger of taking Pitman's Path; Chapter 10 onward shows us how to create the life that we want and how to implement Flipman's Strategy.

I am often asked why I use the name *Flipman*. Originally (and for many years) I used the name Stickman, quite simply because I would draw a stick figure to explain the process to my audiences. One day I was feeling quite frustrated in my attempt to quickly introduce the concept to a new colleague verbally. He just wasn't getting it until I blurted out, "You just flip it. When you're being a Pitman you flip your negative thinking, feeling, and behavior to the opposite." As soon as I saw the instant understanding on his face, I knew the name Flipman was so much more appropriate. Please note that the term "Flipman" is not meant to be gender-specific. The "-man" represents *hu*man. Over the years, people have fondly personalized Flipman. We now have Flip-woman, Flip-chick, Flip-boy, and Flip-girl. Just for commonality (and simplicity!), in this book we will be calling him Flipman.

But first, let's meet Pitman.

Pitman

To fully understand this twosome, let's get a really clear picture of who Pitman is, so that we can instantly recognize him when he wants to play havoc with our life. We can all relate to him. My two sons know all about Pitman (as with Flipman, no specific gender is intended). When

Jackson was little, if I sent him to his room for inappropriate behavior, I would hear him chanting, "I love Pitman! I love Pitman!" Even as a small boy, he knew he was in the Pit—hence, the chanting to annoy me!

So where does Pitman live? In the Pit, of course! But he doesn't live in just any old Pit; he lives in the Pit of Misery! We all know the Pit. It's the place we go to when life seems wretched and lonely, when we feel beaten, when everyone is against us and no one understands us. When we feel isolated and all alone. When it looks like it just won't get any better. We've all been to the Pit, haven't we?

We visit the Pit when we think we haven't got enough money, or when we think we're too fat, too skinny, too lonely, too sad, too tired, or too lost, or when we're just fed up! We go there when we think we're being picked on, left behind, criticized, or pushed too far. We go there when we feel underwhelmed or overwhelmed or even just plain bored. Consequently, we can begin to feel helpless, angry, mean, paranoid, nasty, empty, afraid, and Pitiful—like a victim. It's the place where we feel sorry for ourselves when life gets a little too hard. When we are in the Pit of Misery, we are a living, breathing, walking, talking Pitman! Some of us go to the Pit for an hour, others go there for a day,

and there are many of us who go to the Pit a bit too often and for a bit too long. Some people live their entire life in the Pit. We all go to the Pit; it's how long we stay there that makes all the difference.

One of the most powerful aha! moments that I have ever had was this—if we know how to do Pitman, then we know how to do Flipman. It's exactly the same strategy—we just flip it! Some of us may deny that we consciously set out to create a miserable life, but as we continue this exploration into what it takes to create an empowered life, we will begin to see that it is our habitual, unsupportive behaviors, thoughts, and feelings that keep us in the Pit. And it will be our new conscious behaviors, thoughts, and feelings that create the life we want. Same process—just the opposite outcome.

It's also very important to note at this point that when I talk about Pit behaviors and reactions, I'm *not* talking about *healthy emotions*, such as *grief, sadness, shock, respectful anger*, or *frustration*. Life can be challenging, and we need to be able to express our real feelings when they arise. These are therapeutic emotions that need to be experienced and expressed in order for healing and growth to take place. We've all had our fair share of Pit days—the days when we just want to dive into bed, pull the covers over our head, and hope the rest of the world goes away. The problems arise when we don't move through these emotions. We cling to them and react with bitterness and/or self-pity for the wrongs done to us or by us.

Pit behavior is any behavior that has a negative effect on us or those around us. We make excuses for why we can't act now, so we postpone our life of greatness. Now, if you've just thought to yourself, "Yeah, but you don't know how bad my life is!"—that's serious Pit talk. We need to recognize when we're in the Pit so we can choose to climb out. There are many telltale signs of Pit behavior, and being able to identify them is half the journey. When we're being a Pit person, we take on Pit posture. We walk with our head and shoulders down and with our eyes and mouth downcast—a defeated posture. We tend to walk slowly, dragging our feet behind us. We feel heavy, as if the weight of the world is on our shoulders. Sometimes Pit people even have aggressive body language. They throw their hands in the air, roll their eyes, and give looks that could decalcify a spine at six hundred yards!

You can see a Pit person coming from a mile away. You hope he or she goes the other way, but it doesn't happen. In your cheeriest voice, you ask the question you should never ask if you don't want it answered: "How are you?" His or her shoulders droop further, and he or she replies, "Oh, don't even ask!" Instantly, you can feel your energy being sucked right out of you. When I was in my early twenties, my boss at the time called people like this "energy suckers." What a great term for exactly how we feel when we're around someone who lives his or her life in the Pit. Another friend of mine uses the term "emotional vampire." Suffice to say, we all know what I mean when I say Pit Person.

"What's wrong with this person?" you ask yourself. The answer is usually quite simple! This person has usually made the Pitman state his or her habitual way of life. Remember, we can *all* fall prey to Pitman, and it can happen slowly and seductively. Over time, this "flat" feeling can actually become a habit, and some of us can actually get used to feeling flat or numb. We can get used to having bad posture to the extent that the muscles actually modify into a *hunched* position. There have been many psychological studies on the effects of body posture and emotions. Next time you're feeling down, check your stance. Then do the same the next time you are feeling great. I'm sure you will see that the way you carry yourself is vastly different. How we hold ourselves physically affects how we feel emotionally (as well as vice versa).

Eventually, we can get so used to looking for the downside of life that we cease to notice the fabulous things that are occurring all around us. Later I'll cover how to protect ourselves from falling into Pit habits, but for now, just pay attention to how you carry yourself. Without necessarily realizing it, our carriage tells others a lot about how we may be feeling, even if we're *not* feeling that way. It's interesting to also note that we are not necessarily born as optimistic, happy-go-lucky people. In fact, our brain has been hardwired to expect the worst. In our earlier Neanderthal days, we did not come out of the cave singing, "There's a blue bird on my shoulder!" We ventured out with intense caution and fear. We expected to be attacked by a ferocious animal and killed at any moment. That has been hardwired into our reptilian brain, so it's natural for us to feel pessimistic and negative at times. It's natural for us to have our low days and our tough moments, and it's unnatural to be happy 24/7. So relax—you're normal!

Having said that, it does not serve our goals, or ourselves, if we get stuck in those moments. Living in the NOW is allowing ourselves to feel all of our emotions—the good feelings and the not-so-good feelings—so we can experience them and then release them, thus allowing ourselves to move forward. We don't wait; we get on with doing what needs to be done to create "great." But Pitman does not want us to have that sort of freedom, so it is our responsibility to pay attention when he is lurking around, trying to entice us back into that Pit.

My Pitman comes out on those cold mornings just before my run. He's there with his little face at my window, whispering in his seductive, enticing voice, "It's cold out here, Terry. Stay in bed where you're cozy and warm. You know you're sore and tired. Do it!" It takes all my might to ignore him. Pitman is everywhere. Watch yourself!

Chapter 3

Pit Language and Professional Pit People

When we're being a *Pit person* with our *Pit posture,* we also have *Pit prattle!* Pit prattle is that little voice inside our heads that mutters away to us. If you've just asked yourself, "What voice?"—that's it! Go ahead and introduce yourself! When we're in the Pit, this little voice will grumble in a negative and defeatist way:

"I hate my life."

"How could anyone love me?"

"I'll never be any good."

"I'm so hopeless."

"Why doesn't anyone understand me?"

"I'll never get over this hang-up."

"I'll be lonely all my life."

"I hate my job."

"Why did they do this to me?"

"No one understands me."

"How will I ever cope?"

"Nothing seems to go right for me!"

"I'll never get any better."

"I need more money."

"I can't stand this anymore."

"I'm sick and tired of everything."

"I'll never get out of this hellhole."

"I can't change; I've been this way all my life."

"I'm stuck in this job/relationship/town . . . *blah, blah, blah.*"

Pit prattle is incredibly pessimistic, and when we are allowing our Pitman to rule, we can tend to criticize others and ourselves harshly. Pit dwellers often vocalize their Pit prattle. They constantly complain about their partners, their jobs, their lives, their kids, the traffic, the weather, TV commercials, the price of food, today's youth, today's elderly, last night's dinner, and tomorrow's dessert!

It's as if they can't control themselves, and of course, it's never *their* fault; the fault always lies elsewhere. And if you even attempt to offer a more positive outlook, they'll give you countless reasons why you're wrong. They'll argue on behalf of their limitations and shortfalls, trying to convince you that things are out of their control.

Now, think about *your* habitual responses. How do

you react when it rains? When the kids leave their bags at the front door? When the dog poops inside? (My Pitman comes out when our dogs do that!) When the traffic is heavy? When the train is late? When your new lover doesn't call? When your old lover does?

For most of us, Pitman is just an occasional visitor, but some people are quite comfortable having Pitman around constantly, and he soon becomes a habit, as we discussed earlier. If he sticks around too long, we are in danger of becoming a PPP—a Professional Pit Person! We become so good at telling our Pit story that we start to make it more dramatic, more intense, to the point that we become addicted to our tale and want to hang on to it at all costs.

When we get this serious about being in our Pit, we start renovating. After all, if we're planning on being down there for a while, we might as well make it comfortable, right? You see, PPPs like to have a pretty Pit! Professional Pit People put a lot of time into setting up their Pit. They may even put some furniture in there—a table, maybe some chairs—and a TV and DVD player (they need the technology to play all of those sad movies and sad songs). Heck, if you're going to be really negative, why not build a basement? Why go up when you can go down deep—really, really deep?

Pit Party with Pit Pals

We can also get lonely in our Pit, and as we know, misery loves company, so we end up having a Pit Party with our Pit Pals! Pit Pals are people who get a buzz from feeding off of each other's bad luck stories. Serious Pit dwellers can actually feel disappointed when they meet someone who has had a worse life than theirs!

So how do we dig ourselves out of this Pit? By being aware of the different phrases we use when we're communicating, we can educate ourselves and avoid fueling our situation. Or if we find ourselves giving in to the habit, we can take it as a prompt to turn ourselves around. Here are some examples of Pit talk to be aware of and avoid:

"Nothing ever goes right for me!"

"Can you believe how disgustingly hot it is?"

"Rain always depresses me."

"I'm nothing without him/her."

"I've never been any good at . . ."

"My kids are so annoying."

"I never have time for myself."

"I find it impossible to make friends."

"I wish she/he would grow up."

"I'll never get out of this debt."

"It's OK for you; you don't know how hard it is for me!"

"Why are they doing this to me?"

"Why is this happening to me?"

"What did I do to deserve this?"

"Gosh, you're so annoying."

"Why would you do something that stupid?"

"I wish I had more money."

"I wish I had less stress."

"I wish I didn't have so much work to do."

"I wish I had a new job."

"What is wrong with you?"

"I wish these people would leave me alone."

"I wish I wasn't alone."

"I hate this town, job, relationship, life . . ."

Pulled into the Pit

We have to be very careful when hanging out with people who've made their Pit too cozy, because helping someone who spends a lot of time in the Pit can be very seductive. We all love the warm glow of offering counsel to someone, but are we really helping? When we go down into the Pit with them and start believing that we're the only one who can help them, we're in danger of becoming a rescuer.

We might think at first that we're that special someone who can turn this person's life around. We might even think that it will be *our* wisdom, *our* advice, and *our* guidance that will change him or her. Many of us desperately want to help those we love who have become comfortable in their Pits. We want so much to help that we are in danger of joining them.

A rescuer needs a victim, and a victim needs a rescuer. They are both Pit states; it's just that the rescuer has a better marketing team! Quite often, the rescuer role can feel positive and optimistic, but the positivity is usually for self-gain and not for the long-term success or development of the other person—the more helpless the person, the bigger the rush for the rescuer. The old adage "Give a man a fish, and he'll eat for a day; teach him how to fish, and he'll eat for a lifetime" is a brilliant description of the difference between rescuing and truly helping someone. One creates a dependency; the other teaches us to take personal responsibility for our life. There are many powerful books on the damaging effects of codependency, and most of us have experienced this to some degree in our relationships.

I played the rescuer role for many years. The way that I first began to realize I was rescuing was the telltale rush I would feel when someone came to me with a problem. In those moments, I felt much more significant if I could help the person with his or her issues. It wasn't so much about their problem but more about how wonderful I was for helping them. When I started to see that "saving" them wasn't empowering them, I learned how to effectively coach people through their problems rather than be the rescuer. The outcome was much more powerful and positive, and the people were able to take total responsibility for their life rather than always depending on someone else to solve their issues. *It can be difficult to truly own the answer that someone else gives you.*

No one can help a Pit Person who doesn't *want* to be helped. Sure, we can encourage, guide, and support, but people in a Pit state need to find their own way to climb out. We can't *drag* them to the surface!

In other words, the only person who can save you is YOU!

I recall sitting beside a gentleman at a conference dinner where I had spoken earlier in the day. He said to me that he had been really offended when I first started speaking about the Pit. He thought I was making fun of people who had genuine issues and real struggles in their life, and as he sat there in the audience he felt I was trivializing their problems. He then said that the more he listened, the more he realized that I was actually speaking about his wife! He realized that he had climbed into the Pit with her. He felt incredibly sorry for her yet admitted that he had started finding excuses to stay late at work because he felt so drained when he was around her. He acknowledged that by sympathizing with her, he was helping her to stay in the Pit, and that was why he had reacted so strongly to me on stage. His truth was coming up, and he didn't like it.

Wow! What a realization! He was referring to a form of response in his marriage known as *enabling*. He had made the same mistake a lot of us make when we're trying to help someone in the Pit: he had gone down into the Pit with his wife and was enabling her. When we offer pity to Pit people, we are not helping them. We're simply reinforcing their reasons to remain in the Pit. As we continue to offer great amounts of pity and sympathy to people in their Pit, we give them even more reason to remain in there. We reward them with attention for being a Pit Person!

After first being offended by my presentation, my dinner companion went on to explain that he had confused empathy with sympathy in his dealings with his wife. He felt incredibly guilty about withdrawing from her, and he realized that he was avoiding the situation rather than dealing with it. He was grateful for his new perspective and was inspired to create some changes in his relationship.

Many of us can fall into the trap of being an enabler under the guise of love. I remember a very loving father telling me of the grief he had felt after he had to evict his son from his home. The father had put up with years of his son's drug abuse, unemployment, and apathy. His son contributed nothing to the upkeep of the home, and his lack of gratitude was often displayed in abusive tirades against other members of the family. The father told his son that he loved him with every inch of his being, but he could no longer support him in the destruction of his life and the negative impact he was having on the remainder of the family. He explained that he would be there for his son with love and time, but he needed to end the living arrangement.

I thought how brave this father was; it would have taken an enormous amount of courage to take this action. Then he made a comment that rocked me to my core because of its absolute truth: "Terry, I now realize, after meeting Pitman, that I had to starve my son from the oxygen in that Pit! I was *allowing* him to continue with his behavior, but at the same time I was constantly complaining about it. I was like his Pit dealer!"

Wow! That comment made it clear to me. How often do we enable people who are permanently living in their Pit because we can't deal with the consequences?

From painful firsthand experience, I know that we can wait our entire lives for some loved ones to get out of their Pit. We can pour everything into "helping" them climb out, only to realize years later that little has changed except for the complete depletion of our own energy levels. There's a wonderful line in the Janet Jackson song "Interlude-Full"—"How empty of me to be so full of you"—a brilliant description of how it feels trying to save a Permanent Pit Person.

The man went on to explain that his son started living in his car. The man felt deep guilt as a result, but he also felt completely lost as to what else to do. He stayed committed to his word, and as a result, the son cut off contact for almost a year. This, the man said, was the longest year of his life. That was definitely tough love. But as difficult as it was for him, he didn't wait until it was *too late*; he chose to act *now*.

How easy it is to wait in the seductive hope of the Pit, thinking that the situation will get better, that the person will change, that life will magically transform. But if nothing changes, nothing changes.

One day there was a knock at the door, and there stood his son: clean-shaven, employed, and with his life back on track.

As the father shared this story with me, he had tears in his eyes, especially when he told me how his son said that he knew his father loved him, and it was this love that had motivated him to get his life in order. He had wanted to make his father proud of him again.

Contrast this with another story I recall: a very gruff, aggressive man approaching me after one of my presentations. He said, "I wish my pathetic son could hear you speak. He's totally hopeless! He's eighteen, unemployed, smokes dope, lies on the couch all day, and is just throwing his life away. He's a complete waste of space."

Here we have the same situation, yet this father was stuck in criticism instead of resolution. I'm sure he thought he was trying to help, but attacking people personally is never helpful. I'm not condoning the son's behavior, but constant criticism is often a contributing factor to keeping an individual in this state. I would never call my children naughty or bratty. When we use terms like this, we are judging the whole child instead of isolating the specific behavior. I think my son Harison explained this to me perfectly when he was three years old. A gecko was sitting in the middle of the garden step, and I said, "Look at that silly gecko!"

Harison replied wisely, "Mumma, he isn't a silly gecko; he just does silly things sometimes." It is empowering to know that we are *not* our behaviors and that we're valuable as human beings regardless of what we do.

Let's all pay attention to the language that's used to keep people in the Pit. We usually get the behavior that we keep reinforcing. I remember being overly critical of Harison as a young teenager, and he once again wisely said, "Mum, do you really think calling me that is going to make me want to change?" I ate humble pie and apologized. None of us *are* our behaviors, and that's why we *can* change the way we *do* our life if it isn't serving us. I can give you countless stories of people (including myself) who have lived part or all of their lives in the Pit, either in a rescuing role, as a victim, or both. When we have the courage to stop rescuing or playing the victim, the Pit dance stops. When one of you decides to stop the negative routine, the other person is faced with a choice: either learn a new, more positive dance or stay in the Pit and find a new Pit partner.

However, for some of us, owning our happiness can create an internal conflict. Do we risk what we have, even if it isn't serving us? I hear it all the time from unhappy lovers, discouraged employers, and disgruntled employees. I hear it from lots of people who are unhappy with their relationships but are not willing to *do* anything about it.

Even when we are willing to do something, we have to remember the importance of *how* we do it. That's why learning the difference between sympathy and empathy is critical.

Chapter 4

It's Not Always about You!

I don't think we spend enough time understanding the power of empathy and sympathy and the effect that these two states have on our perception. Sympathy can be very seductive and can easily keep us in the Pit if we're not careful. Sometimes we even want to throw a blanket in and have a Pit Pity Day, which is fine, as long as we don't get seduced into staying for too long. Remember, it's easy to become stuck in the habit of Pit behavior.

Empathy is a simple word, and one of the most understated, underused, and undervalued words in our language. I once heard the difference between empathy and sympathy described this way: *Sympathy is when you join people in their dark place (the Pit), and empathy is when you throw them a ladder.* When we come from a place of empathy, we give people permission to be whatever they need to be, and we are better able to support them in an objective way. Expressing empathy is also a powerful way to release anguish from the past and to connect with others in the present.

Empathy is having the ability to put yourself in someone else's shoes and see things as they do. This Native American proverb depicts it beautifully: *Don't judge any man until you have walked two moons in his moccasins.*

Empathy is the ability to understand another person's thoughts, feelings, and opinions. Empathy refrains from passing judgment and avoids categorizing a person as being right or wrong. It's the ability to use your imaginative skills to see a situation as the other person does — *not* "If I were you, I would . . ."

Being empathic sounds simple in theory, but it's one of the most difficult states to put ourselves in. If it were easy, we would have fewer wars, less conflict, fewer divorces, and less aggression in the world. The power of empathy is so great that I believe if we all made it our daily practice, we would go a long way toward creating a world filled with much more peace and harmony. In its most powerful form, empathy precedes forgiveness — for when we truly understand, how can we not forgive?

Empathy does *not* mean we have to agree with someone when we really don't — it's about giving ourselves permission to see the situation as the other person does. Let's take a four-sided house, with each of its outer walls a different strong color: red, yellow, green, or blue. Now let's take four people and place each one in front of a different side of the house, so they can't see any other sides. If I were to ask each individual the color of the house, what would they say? With absolute conviction, they would say either red, yellow, green, or blue. Are they all right? Yes! Because *their* view of the house is of that color. It is only red, yellow, blue, or green to them; that is all they see. This is such a powerful metaphor—if we get it. When we are too quick to denounce another's opinion because it doesn't fit our current reality (our view of the house), we stop all new learning from occurring. Sometimes it's wise to just "sit" with new concepts, ideas, and opinions and just contemplate—consider the possibility. Our way is just one way, not *the* way. When we become consumed with proving that we are right, we stop our own evolution. Be open to the power of thinking in a different way: seeing with different eyes, feeling with a different heart, and letting go of what no longer serves you.

Empathy is a fascinating state of being. Most of us intellectualize empathy, but it can be very challenging to actually integrate empathy into our being. To intellectualize something is to stand separate from it and observe it. We see what it is, but we don't necessarily experience "being" what it is. Integration means really living it, making it part of our DNA. When we integrate empathy, we move from a conscious state into an unconscious state; it becomes part of *who* we are rather than part of what we do.

We all want to think that we're incredibly empathic. I'm sure you're probably the most empathic person you know! So let's put your empathy muscle to the test, shall we?

There you are, driving in the traffic, enjoying yourself, maybe even grooving to your favorite tune, when suddenly another car comes out of nowhere and abruptly cuts in front of you! You slam on the brakes, you swerve to avoid a collision, and the whole thing feels like a near-death experience. As you push your heart back down your throat, you roll down your window and say in a calm voice, "I completely understand your situation. You probably didn't see me. Are you OK?"

Yeah, right! This is why car horns were invented!

I'm sure the majority of us see ourselves as caring, loving, enthusiastic, compassionate, and kind people. However, *being* those traits is a completely different thing.

Let's try another situation. You arrive home in the evening to greet your partner. You've had a great day, and in you walk. "Hi, honey! I'm home!" you say in your cheeriest voice. All you get in response is a miserable grunt.

"Oh, darling," you respond. "You don't seem to be your normal happy self. What's up, sugar plum?"

Your partner replies, "Oh, I'm so sorry, darling, I'm just not feeling well. Come on, give me a hug!"

As if!

It probably goes more like this:

YOU: Hi, honey!

PARTNER: *(Grunt)*

YOU: What's wrong?

PARTNER: Nothing's wrong!

YOU: Then why are you snapping at me?

PARTNER: I'm not snapping at you! Just because I'm not all over you doesn't mean there's something wrong!

YOU: Why do you always have to be so grumpy?

And before you know it, an argument erupts.

Sometimes we think we're being empathic when we're actually falling into an automatic sympathetic state. We can easily confuse sympathy with empathy. Being sympathetic means we take on the feelings and behaviors of the other person, or we move into a state of feeling sorry for the person or ourselves. Sympathy can even lead to our responding in a condescending manner.

We feel sorry for the others, or we buy into their sadness, hurt, anger, frustration, pain, and so on, after which we tend to mirror that behavior. It goes like this: They're angry, so we become angry. They're sad, so we get sad. They're frustrated, so we switch to frustration. They're cranky, so we get cranky too.

Have you ever had a friend, spouse, lover, or family member talk to you about a situation, and you go straight into feeling what they feel? It's easy to do. For example, they tell you about a situation at work where they feel that someone has been picking on them. We usually go straight into defending our loved one and condemning the work colleague. We say, "Oh, you poor thing, I feel so sorry for you." We may think we're comforting them, but we're actually offering a false sense of comfort. If anything, sympathy can make the person feel more frightened, more lonely, and worse.

Sympathy can also be a self-centered reaction, because our response is usually based on how *we* would feel if something like that happened to us. Sympathetic love is a victim state; it's an enabling state; it's a "feel sorry for" state.

In contrast, empathy is not about us — it is completely about the other person. When we have true empathy, we don't cloud the situation with our feelings, thoughts, and opinions. We use our imaginative skills to picture what it must be like for *the other person* to experience this situation.

The great thing about being empathic is that it stops us from assuming, which then gives us the chance to ask questions. So often we interpret situations based on our own perceptions—only to find out that we're completely out of sync with how the other person *really* feels. When we put ourselves in the picture, we pollute it with our interpretation. We pollute it with our values; we pollute it with our bias. We pollute it with our beliefs, our temperament, our age, our gender, our past experiences, our cultural background, our financial position, our education, and our religious views. We pollute our perception by filtering it through all of these and more. This prevents us from seeing any view other than our own.

When we're in an empathic state and we're imagining what it's like for someone else, we are not part of their picture. The easiest way to determine whether you're being empathic in its purest form is to ask yourself, "Am I seeing their picture or have I created my own picture? Am I basing this on their filters or mine?" Unfortunately, we often *do* create our own picture of their story. For example, someone describes a situation to us, or we see a story on the news, and our response becomes, "I understand how that person must be feeling, because when *I'm* in that situation, I feel . . ." We assume that the person is going to have the same reaction that we would. This is not being empathic; this is putting our personal judgments, interpretations, and values onto the other person. Empathy is always about remaining completely neutral. Yes, relating to a situation from our own past experience can give us a deeper understanding or a good reference point, but it is important to remember not to pollute their experience with our own. When we're empathic, we don't necessarily agree. We just see. We see it through the "eyes" of another.

There was an uproar many years ago about wild baby seal pups being killed, and as much as I disagree with killing innocent animals, I could understand that the killing was a form of livelihood for those doing the killing. I could see the situation from the other side only when I put my emotional reaction on pause. Of course, I could never imagine myself, with my lifestyle, killing helpless baby animals—but if I imagine being a father desperate to earn money to feed my hungry children, then yes, I can see how it is possible.

If you *really* get empathy, I promise you that many parts of your life will manifest into abundance, and you'll experience a new sense of calm and compassion. The more you practice empathy in all parts of your life, the more you'll integrate it into your everyday manner. For example, in business, imagine if you were to exist in a state of empathy with your clients. Imagine that you didn't worry about making money, or hitting targets, or how you looked, and that you remained purely and objectively focused on that client and the client's needs. You would sell more than you could ever imagine to customers who would truly appreciate you and your service. When we really step into the shoes of the customer and wear their eyes, ears, and emotions for a moment, we create a connection that's trusting and real. People respond to that because they feel significant. It isn't an intellectual or calculated response; it's a genuine display of concern and caring.

Now let's take empathy from a relationship point of view. If we were totally empathic with the people we're in relationships with, it wouldn't be about us. It wouldn't be about our gain; it wouldn't be about what we did or didn't get out of it. It would be about how we could serve the person we were with. If that person had the same intention, can you imagine the harmony within the relationship? It would be amazing! Whatever we want for ourselves is usually a good indicator of what we should give first to another; what we give, we usually receive.

Of course, in any relationship, issues will come up and conflict will occur, but if we could come from the point of view of the other person first and really aim to see things through that person's eyes *before* we state our case, we would have a far greater chance of a more peaceful and harmonious union. Whether we're leading someone, loving someone, listening to someone, or serving someone, if we come from an empathic base, we're on course to creating a successful and meaningful relationship. Being empathic with another human being isn't easy, though, and that's why few people do it authentically. Yet when we put the focus on truly wanting to understand the person before us, wonderful things can happen.

I met a lovely man after one of my conferences. The section in my presentation on empathy had moved him greatly. He mentioned that he was having trouble connecting with his fifteen-year-old daughter, and they seemed to be growing apart. She rarely spent time with him, unlike his older daughter, who seemed to enjoy the same things he did. This father really wanted to work on their relationship, but everything he tried to do seemed to push his daughter away even more.

As he spoke, I could see tears in his eyes. I asked him if he had honestly told his daughter how he was *feeling*—how much he loved her and that he wanted to get closer to her—instead of just analyzing why they weren't connecting. He said they had never discussed these matters, and he resolved to do so at the earliest opportunity.

I received an e-mail from him a few days later saying that he had sat his daughter down and told her how he understood that she was growing up and finding her own interests. He explained to her that as much as he was proud of her finding her own identity, this appeared to have an effect on how much time they spent together, and there was a distance growing between them. He explained that he quite simply just missed being with her. He also told her he didn't have any answers but just wanted her to know how much he wanted to be closer to her, and he loved her with all his heart. He told her the beautiful, honest truth about his own vulnerability—not that she was wrong or what he expected from her or their relationship.

Once he opened up and showed his sensitivity without judging his daughter, she also became empathic. She saw how they had drifted apart and how that must have hurt him. She also confessed that she was a little jealous of the relationship he had with her older sibling. They cried, hugged, and agreed to spend more time getting to know each other. This brave father and daughter proceeded on a wonderful journey of creating a great relationship based on understanding and love, not judgment, mind reading, and false expectations.

It's easy to find ourselves wanting everyone else to understand *us* so that our needs get filled first, especially when we're overwhelmed with life. But if we all were to make the effort to discover the uniqueness of those we share our lives with, we would be amazed at how much easier our communication could be. Empathy is completely about the other person, and it's the key to helping us understand the people we live with.

My two sons are different in many ways—from their temperament and personality, to the way they explain something, to what they do in their spare time, to the music they enjoy. That's because they *are* different, and my job as their parent is to invest the time to work out what motivates them, what drives them, and how they think and feel so that I can support them the best I can in *their* journey. I parent them each very differently because of this, and along the way I explain their differences to each of them so that they, too, can grow up realizing that people *are* different and that's OK. When we understand that we are all different, we begin to appreciate that our reactions and emotions are also different.

Chapter 5

Genuine Emotion Is Not the Pit

As I said earlier—and I can't stress this too much—Pit behaviors and reactions *do not include healthy emotions*, such as *grief, sadness, shock, respectful anger*, or *frustration*. As we all know, life can throw us many curveballs, and we humans are designed to deal with the stress of life through feeling and expressing our emotional responses to these events. Crying, for example, is such a healing act; it allows our body to release the sadness we are holding. I cringe when I hear parents tell their children (especially their young boys) to stop crying when they are sad. I admire anybody who can be brave and strong enough to be in their vulnerability and allow the emotions to rise and be expressed. Strength is not the ability to *not* cry; it's the ability *to* cry, to laugh, to be scared, to be brave, to communicate respectful anger and frustration—to feel and express those feelings.

Too often, we push these important emotions down because we become fearful of really experiencing and *feeling* them. We can start to believe that the pain in our chest is too much to bear, so we stop—we wait. But we are meant to feel. Our hearts are meant to be broken, but they never break in two—they just break open to allow us to love more and feel even more. However, getting to this understanding can be a real test—sometimes it can seem much easier just to push it all down and instead become bitter and resentful. When we do this, our Pit emotions come to the surface and we end up spraying our *Pit Pollution* onto everyone, with our Pitman behaviors and comments.

Sometimes our memories can be so painful that we don't allow ourselves the necessary emotional expression vital for healing. We shut the memories away, hoping the pain will go with them. But where do they go? They can't just disappear. Could it be that we somehow unconsciously redirect our unexpressed emotions? Unlike some people, who can become emotionally addicted to the event by playing it over and over in their heads, others can shut down the memory, transmuting it into other addictions (subaddictions) such as food, alcohol, anger, sex, drugs, or work.

If I could leave a legacy, it would be to have helped people *do pain well*. Not to go around pain, not to manage pain, and not to cope with pain, but to go into the eye of the pain, experience it, and then let it pass through. I believe when we learn how to master that, we won't resist our feelings, and we will arrive at peace. Peace to me is not a sense of calm, but a sense of knowingness—that regardless of what comes our way, we will be OK.

Unfortunately, though, we can spend so much of our energy, time, and resources trying to do whatever we can to avoid pain that we end up numbing ourselves with everything we can lay our hands on, just so we can avoid discomfort. The irony, however, is that the very pain we are trying to avoid is the very vehicle that will set us free.

A good example of the difference between allowing yourself to pass through your emotions and getting stuck in the Pit comes from a friend of mine. Her husband died tragically in a car accident, and a few weeks afterward she called me to announce she had gone to the Pit for the night.

She said that she reread all the sympathy cards she received and had a big cry. I explained to her this was a really healthy thing to do and she wasn't in the Pit at all. She was grieving, and it was important for her emotional healing to release her feelings. I encouraged her to cry whenever she felt the need. In my children's books, I encourage children to "cry and cry and cry until there is no more cry left!"

A few weeks passed, and she called me again. This time, her conversation went something like this: "I can't cope. I had to drop the kids off at school, deliver a pile of brochures, bring the car in for service, get back to pick up the car in time to get the kids, and then they started fighting. It's all too much!"

That's when I said, "OK, *now* you're in the Pit!" and we laughed.

The Pit is that place we go to when we think we don't have any power. It's where we blame everyone and everything for where we're at. When we feel like this, we tend to generate a powerful force that sucks the energy out of anyone who projects a positive outlook. I know exactly when I'm being a Pit dweller, because I can see the effect it has on me and the effect I have on others. I have less energy and less patience; I am quicker to anger and to criticize. I see this reflected on the faces of those who have to experience my Pit Pollution. I have also realized that for me, these "triggers" were simply indicators that I wasn't allowing my true feelings to rise — my anger, for example, was often a cover-up for my wanting to cry or express my fear.

Chapter 6

Gaining the Courage to Feel

We can spend our entire lives running away from certain memories, trying to avoid the pain they trigger. We commit vast amounts of energy and effort to trying to forget our painful past, but in reality, the pain associated with avoiding these feelings is usually far greater than the pain of confronting them. This avoidance can also manifest as something else in our future, something that doesn't support us in leading a healthy, fulfilled life.

A few years ago, my dearest girlfriend lost her precious husband — a big, bold, and brilliant man, the father of her four children — in a farming accident. His sudden departure ripped their world apart, and their grief was torture to witness. During my visit, I overheard a friend of my girlfriend giving her some advice: "Come on. Be strong. You can't let the kids see you falling apart." I had to hold my tongue — I knew her friend had the best of intentions, but her advice was terribly misguided.

Later that day I explained to my beautiful friend that it was really important and healthy to express all of her pain and grief, and that by doing so she would be giving her children permission to express whatever they needed to, to move through their own grief. I explained that if they didn't allow these vital healing emotions to arise and come out, their unexpressed pain and sadness would find another way out, perhaps much later in life. It might present itself as an inability to create trusting relationships, or unwarranted anger with a child of their own, perhaps as an unexplained detachment with a spouse, or as a variety of other "unexplained" outbursts. What we don't deal with now will almost certainly come back to visit us later.

We all have something from our past that shakes our center and puts a spin on how we see the world. It's a story that we define ourselves by; a story that we allow to influence everything in our life. The question is: does it have to control our life forever? No!

We cannot change the past, and we cannot change anything that has happened to us. However, we *do* have the power to change our perceptions of these events and our responses to them, and that can affect our present and our future. It's about redefining our memories so they serve us well for all the todays and all the tomorrows we still have left to live.

When we relive the past as if it's still happening, we react with the same intense feelings as if we were back in the experience all over again. We revisit the same hurtful memories as if, by some miracle, *this time* we'll feel differently. But that won't happen unless we're *willing to remember it differently*—and that takes courage, contemplation, and, perhaps, forgiveness. When we've reached the point where we've cried enough, hurt enough, been angry enough, or grieved enough, it becomes time for us to move forward without the weight of these past experiences.

I really want to stress how important it is to make the decision to *want* to let it go. Old harmful memories don't make us feel good, but their familiarity keeps us going back to them. Until we decide to let them go, everything that I'm about to say will seem either too simple or too frivolous.

The strategy for releasing or redesigning our past memories so that they serve us for our future is relatively easy to understand. Actually *undertaking* the process can be more challenging.

The place to start is accepting that it is neither the experiences nor the people in our lives that cause us pain; it is the *meaning* we have placed on these experiences that creates our anguish. Please understand that I'm not trivializing the pain we feel at the time nor the trauma we may feel when we remember these past events, whether another person inflicted them or it's from a regret we still cling to. And I'm not saying that with a single effort we can make all of our pain disappear. I just want you to consider the possibility that we *continue to carry the pain* because of how we now perceive it, and that there is a way to set down the burden of our past and reap the learning that can set us free. That's my wish here — that we no longer stay wrapped in the chains of memories that keep us sad, fearful, closed, resentful, guilty, remorseful, bitter, or persecuted.

So if we are to dare to make our way down this path of releasing our pain, I invite you to courageously consider this statement: *Our past does not hurt us.* The pain comes from the meaning we ascribe to the experience, and this creates the hurt we feel in the present as well. If we can change the way we perceive these experiences (and thus change the meaning we have given them), we have a very good chance of being able to change the feelings we have created about these past experiences. When we change our perceptions, our brain responds to those changes biologically, and our feelings change as a result.

How Thoughts Become Real

In their book *Words Can Change Your Brain*, Andrew Newberg, M.D., and Mark Robert Waldman talk about the role of the thalamus in influencing our physiological response to our perceptions.

> In the center of our brain there's a walnut-shaped structure called the thalamus. It relays sensory information about the outside world to the other parts of the brain. When we imagine something, this information is also sent to the thalamus. Our research suggests that the thalamus treats these thoughts and fantasies in the same way it processes sounds, smells, tastes, images, and touch. And it doesn't distinguish between inner and outer realities. Thus, if you think you are safe, the rest of your brain assumes that you are safe. But if you ruminate on imaginary fears or self-doubt, your brain presumes that there may be a real threat in the outside world. Our language-based thoughts shape our consciousness, and consciousness

shapes the reality we perceive. So choose your words wisely, because they become as real as the ground on which you stand.

A perfect example of this is when a child tells herself there is a monster in her closet. She starts to panic, her heart races, and she may even cry. But as soon as she opens the closet door and finds there are no monsters to be seen, she immediately begins to calm down and relax. Her heartbeat returns to normal and her tears dry up.

Now, if you think this sounds way too easy, let me explain. Think about a difficult situation in your past. Every time you recall that memory, do you experience a painful emotion? Is it grief? Embarrassment? Shame? Guilt? Betrayal? Disappointment? Regret? Disgust? Dismay? Fear? Sadness? Anger? Resentment? Revenge? Bitterness? Pity?

Of course, in the initial stages of an experience, or during the grieving or healing process, certain emotions are vital. We need to feel all of our emotions initially before we can move on to finding the gifts of wisdom. But why is it that when we recall a particular incident from years, sometimes decades, past, we still have the same intensity of feeling as we felt at the time it happened? Why do we keep believing the "monster" is still in our closet?

We can get so locked in, so addicted to the emotion of an incident, that we can spend our lifetime replaying the event—and the feeling. We don't move on to experience wisdom. We can spend a lifetime getting over something that happened to us for ten minutes when we were five years old. Sometimes we also allow these events to

Two men in jail,
looking through the bars;
one sees mud,
and the other sees the stars.

negatively affect our decisions in the present, keeping those around us hostage to something we are afraid of or haven't managed to deal with. Instead of bringing forward wisdom, we carry forward the pain and hurt.

This usually happens because we are in an *associated state* when we recall the memory. When we are in an associated state, we imagine ourselves to be in the actual experience; it's as if we are right back there in the moment, and we have the same feelings. We relive that past event as if it is actually happening right now, in the present.

What if you were to change the way you perceive a painful situation from your past? We can do this through dissociation. When we are *dissociated*, we can release the emotional attachment. Therefore the feeling is more of a detached sensation, and over time the emotion can dissipate or even disappear.

The easiest way to do this is to imagine you're looking at yourself on a movie screen and the particular event is playing out before your eyes. You are watching yourself and hearing all the dialogue, yet you feel detached (or dissociated). We do this all the time when we watch a movie, at home or at the cinema. We are seeing it in the third person, so we get to see the entire picture, not just what it looks like through the eyes of one character. This exercise gives us a chance to see the big picture, and we are just one of the characters that make up the entire movie. This counteracts the "poor me" story we tell ourselves and gives us a far more empowering and freeing experience of it.

This can be an extremely healing exercise. It can support us in finding the wisdom from these painful events. As you watch yourself in this event on the imaginary screen, see if you can detach yourself from it. At first this may seem impossible, because we can be so attached to our familiar reactions to the event. Some of us have spent many years compounding our response to the painful memory, so at first we may resist allowing ourselves to see it in the third person.

Sometimes we may also think that by doing this exercise we are somehow condoning the action. I can't stress too much that this is not the case at all. We are simply looking at it from a different angle, a more empowering angle. Nothing is going to change the event, but how we perceive it could change everything internally.

A woman once shared with me that she had been aggressively raped by her father for many years, and when she first started to do this exercise, she didn't know how to be detached because she was so used to her highly charged reaction. She had even stopped herself from thinking about it because of the pain she felt every time. But she persisted with the exercise, and slowly, over time, she was able to look at the event in the third person. She was able to "see" that she wasn't at fault and that she was just a little girl who had learned how to function extremely well regardless of what had happened to her. She was able to realize that she had developed great courage and compassion for others in similar situations.

For the first time, she saw her father as "a pitiful victim of his own childhood abuse" and not the monster that had continued to haunt her all these years later. She continued to be estranged from him, but her feeling of personal empowerment changed completely. For me, the most profound moment in her story was when she said, "Terry, I no longer waste any more of my life on those memories of my life. I feel free." She gave *me* the courage to keep redesigning my memories and rewriting my stories — especially the ones that I had become really addicted to.

If you, too, find this process difficult at first, and you experience an intense emotional reaction, I strongly urge you to journal your thoughts. Start writing about your feelings and what comes to your mind. Keep writing until you're empty of thoughts. Then take a break, go for a walk, have a rest, have a cry, and after you've given yourself some space, reread the journal as if you were reading a story about someone else's life. This may help you to become dissociated. If you find both exercises too overwhelming, give yourself another break and realize that you are one step closer to being able to dissociate.

It can also be of benefit to discuss some of our more painful issues with a counselor or therapist. Having a neutral sounding board can be highly beneficial; it can help us to hold the situation outside of ourselves for long enough to "look" at it.

If you were able to complete the earlier movie exercise, ask yourself: "What did I learn from this experience? If I were to tell the person on the screen what was gained from this experience, what would I say to him or her? What did I learn as a result?" When we open ourselves up to the possibility of allowing our great inner wisdom to surface, we see how these events present us with the opportunity to connect with the greatness that has grown within us as a result. These gifts of wisdom come in many forms and can include the following:

Compassion

Forgiveness

Courage

Insight

Patience

Respect

Integrity

Humility

Sensitivity

Understanding

Love

Surrender

Gratitude

Tenderness

A better way to handle the problem

Empathy

Humor

When we visualize the place in our past that offers us the learning from that painful experience, we can see that regardless of the pain, this experience *has* provided us with an increased depth of wisdom and understanding.

Furthermore, as we reassess its meaning, we will notice our feelings about the event changing over time. Some will notice a shift in their reaction in that very moment. The more committed we are to redesigning the memory, the more significant and long-lasting the change will be at a cellular level. Even though we still may be affected by these memories, we no longer allow our emotions to paralyze and restrain us from moving forward.

I realize that reviewing painful events in this way can feel like something we'd want to avoid at first. While we may find ourselves stuck in those past events, we certainly don't want to be, and most of us do not relish revisiting unpleasant emotions. To find the benefit, we have to face the obstacle. I remember a scene in a war movie: immediately before going into battle, a soldier confessed to his superior officer, "I don't think I should be telling you this, but I'm terrified." The officer wisely replied, "Oh, did they forget to tell you at boot camp? Courage only comes after you have faced the fear." The courage doesn't come first.

Over the years I have been blessed to have many of my workshop participants share their stories with me. One lady in particular—a very gentle, soft-spoken woman—

came up to me and told me how her adult son had been sexually abused at the age of nine. Instantly, my heart ached for her and for her boy. She then told me her greatest personal pain was that she, too, had been abused as a child, and not even this awareness had helped her protect her son.

Her greatest anguish came from not safeguarding the most precious part of her child's life, his innocence. She went on to tell me that although they experienced much pain and sadness together, they also shared a feeling of freedom and bonding. Her son's honesty allowed her to share with him her "dark" past (as she put it). This opening up of truth allowed mother and son to begin their healing process together. After they had moved through the painful yet necessary grieving process, they then were able to look at their experiences in a dissociated state.

It's important to note that this exercise is not intended as a replacement for grief. When we try to do that, we are simply pushing down our feelings, as we discussed earlier, and that's the last thing you want to do. One of the most enriching acts we can do for ourselves is to feel all of our feelings—fully. Then we can move into the phase of receiving the gifts of wisdom. I think we've established a false concept of how long it takes to heal from emotional events. I'm not saying that certain losses, such as the death of a child or a spouse, won't have an effect on us forever, but too often I've seen the surviving parent or spouse "die" as well. They spend the rest of their lives in a grieving state, somehow thinking that perhaps this will show the one they lost that they haven't forgotten them.

I knew of a woman who lost her beautiful eighteen-month-old baby girl to leukemia. I can't imagine the grief and sorrow that filled this young family. But now, ten years on, she still grieves as if it happened yesterday, and her two other beautiful children are stifled by her overprotective fear that they, too, will lose their lives. She has this emptiness about her, and her gorgeous kids get only half a mother. I don't know what it's like to lose a child, and God forbid I ever have to, but I do know what loss is like. An eight-year-old girl described it to me beautifully one day. She said, "Terry, I am scared that if I don't stay sad about my pony dying, people will think I don't love him anymore, so that's why I need to stay sad." We have to give ourselves permission to move on — not to stop loving, but to open our heart to love again. Can you imagine how it would make those lost loved ones feel if they knew that not only had *their* life ended, but so had ours? The greatest respect we can pay to those who have passed is to live a full and passionate life, to give up the guilt and celebrate what we have. I'm sure if this lovely mother were able to dissociate just for a while to watch the movie of her life, she would see how she is shortchanging herself and all three of her beautiful children.

These aren't just words on a page; I've had to live with my own personal challenges as well. I know how hard it can be. One of the personal challenges in my life was experiencing sexual abuse many times as a young child. For many years I allowed myself to feel shattered by those incidents, along with many other traumatic experiences that life thrust upon me. Each time I revisited those memories,

I clung to the pain they had brought me. Interestingly enough, it wasn't the physical aspect that affected me the most; it was the betrayal of trust, the deep confusion and shame I felt, and the longing for it to have been different.

As I have mentioned, I have two beautiful sons, Harison and Jackson. Shortly before Harison's birth, I heard someone speaking about how changing the meaning of a situation will change our feelings about it.

At first, I was angry to hear these dismissive words. How could anyone speak so flippantly and suggest that I could change how I felt about a situation simply by changing the way I thought about it? Didn't they know the pain I had endured? Didn't they know the repercussions of such events and how they had tainted nearly every part of my life? Something was stinging inside (the truth!), so I knew some issue had surfaced for me. It was time to *pay attention*. It was time to really *listen*. As those words rang in my ears, I decided to ponder this new concept.

> What if I did change the meaning I had placed on those experiences?
>
> What if I were to look at them differently and detach myself from my usual highly charged reaction?

I thought about my new baby, soon to come into the world, and then I thought about the advice I would have given to that little girl who was me, all those years ago. I thought about how I could turn the painful memories into powerful learning experiences. I forced myself to give up the anger and resentment so that I could find the wisdom. I decided to redesign my memories around those events.

I learned to avoid perpetuating the negative feelings that resulted from the abuse by now saying that I had "experienced" it, not that I had "suffered" or "survived."

I learned that we are all victims of victims, and that people who are hurting in turn hurt other people. Empathy allowed me to see that. Not agree with it, but see!

I learned that I had an opportunity to teach my children how to protect their bodies; I had the chance to stop the cycle of abuse.

I learned that we have to get past our own discomfort with having these uncomfortable conversations and love our kids enough to help them be aware.

I learned that children need to first be able to recognize a potentially dangerous situation, and then, if they are ever placed in one, to respond automatically—a defense that definitely would have helped me. It's ridiculous to say to kids, "Don't talk to strangers," because we make them talk to strangers every day ("Say hello to Mrs. Smith"). And "Don't accept a lift from someone you don't know" isn't totally foolproof advice, because abusers are very clever at tricking children into trusting them.

We have to give our children responses that we calmly, persistently drill into them so that, should they ever find themselves in such a situation, they are not powerless. Again, that certainly would have helped me. No one told me that it was OK for me to stand up to people who were going to do "bad" things to me. I was so young that I didn't even know they were bad at first, let alone recognize that I was in danger. But even very young children may get a "funny feeling," and if they do, it's this *feeling* that could save them from a predator. You can't *expect* children to get this feeling or to act on it; hence the need to prepare them and to follow up.

So I decided to change the meaning I had placed on my sexual abuse experiences. I changed my outlook from "victimhood" to "empowerment." I realized that those experiences of abuse had given me the insight to teach my children how to protect themselves and how to trust and act on that "funny feeling."

I am also very grateful that I was able to move through the pain to reach the other side, where I could be in a position to teach them what to say and do if they were ever placed in that awful predicament. My children were drilled every week: "If someone tries to touch you or your penis, what do you say and do?" In a really loud, strong voice, they would yell, "No! Go away! I don't know you!" And then they would know to run to me or another woman and tell them what had happened. (Only a very small percentage of child sexual abusers are women.)

My abusers were trusted people in my life, so just limiting this education to cautions about strangers was not enough. I was also adamant about teaching my boys that they had "NO GO" zones on their body, and that absolutely no one could touch them there. I explained to them that even people we know can do bad things to us and then tell us to keep it a secret, but the biggest secret of all is that kids can tell their mothers anything — even secrets. I made sure that we kept having this conversation even as they got older, to make sure they maintained their awareness of their right to protect their body. Pedophiles test, establish trust, and gain their victims' confidence before any inappropriate touching, and then they proceed very gradually. This is called "grooming," and it can happen any time, anywhere, with people you might never suspect. When our children can recognize that certain behavior is *not* acceptable—from anyone—they have a much better chance of protecting themselves. We must give them the resources to take action before they are harmed, not just after. We must give them an instant, default response. This is not just for potential abuse situations, of course; by age three-and-a-half, my boys could say their name, address, phone number, and their doctor's name. They would recite it over and over. It's amazing how many five-year-olds don't even know their own phone number.

So through some very painful personal experiences, I learned something of value that I was able to pass on to my children. There is great wisdom in every experience if we just look for it. I want all of us to let go of the shame and negativity that paralyzes us into waiting to be great. I want us to celebrate the insights gleaned from the journey that has brought us to where we are today.

I didn't want to continue giving my life away to the past, and I wanted to stop feeling like I was "damaged goods" and less than others because of all that had happened to me. My version of hell is getting to the end of my life and someone saying, "*This* is the life you were *supposed* to live! *This* is what you could have done had you not been so stuck in your pain!" I didn't want to waste another moment of my life, and if that meant redesigning how I perceived those events, then so be it! When we realize that no one is broken, no one is damaged, and no one is dysfunctional, we start to accept that our path, whatever it may be and however painful it may have been, has been a great teacher, guiding us to our most wise and connected self.

I have spoken many times with a wonderfully gifted speaker and truly great man, Li Cunxin, the author of *Mao's Last Dancer*. Li was born into utter poverty in Mao's communist China, and at the age of eleven he was selected to train in Madame Mao's Beijing Dance Academy. During his time there he suffered great emotional and physical pain. I recall Li sharing a story from his childhood. One of his mentors told him, "When the heart is breaking with sorrow for what it has lost, the soul is singing with joy for what it has gained." That is a profound insight, and sometimes when I'm feeling great pity for myself, I remind myself of this healing wisdom. It takes great courage to sit in such a place and allow ourselves to get the great learnings from our pain.

Other Ways to Change Perceptions

By changing the meaning we place on situations, we can start to see a way into our wisdom, to peace and to release. We might choose to seek counsel so that we can "see" our past differently. We might also choose to spend time with someone who has experienced a similar problem, as it can help open our eyes to a different perception.

We all have a lot to share, and there are so many opportunities for us to help while healing:

- ► If you experienced sexual abuse, become a hospital volunteer with children who have been sexually abused

- If you were physically, mentally, or intell
  abused, go work with disadvantaged youth.

- If you hated the poverty of your past, serve at a   p
  kitchen one day a month, or hand out dignity packs
  to those who have found themselves homeless.

- If you hated your parents' working, go work at an
  orphanage.

When we step outside of the picture of our own past and see firsthand someone playing the cards they were dealt in a positive way, we begin to understand that our past doesn't have to be the life sentence we have turned it into. I recall a conversation with a participant in one of my programs many years ago, a compassionate young woman with whom I had worked a year or so before. Little did I realize that throughout the first program she'd held a shocking secret. Our conversation went something like this:

"Terry, I've really gained a lot from doing volunteer work. It's helped me to get over the pain of what happened to me."

"What happened to you?"

"Two years ago, I was abducted by a group of young men, kept in the trunk of their car, and continuously raped for a week."

I still get a chill when I recall that conversation. I don't think many of us could even comprehend such a terrifying experience, let alone move on with our life to help those less fortunate. I am reminded of Isaac Newton's observation, "If I have seen further, it is by standing on the shoulders of giants." By overcoming her past, this wonderful girl became a giant for us all. She didn't allow the trauma of that terrible experience to paralyze her. She grieved, she ached, she cried for a long time, she did lots of healing, and then she moved to a place in her soul that could help her to ease other people's pain.

Is this hard to fathom? Some may think, "It can't be that easy." A woman in one of my training sessions held that view. "It's not that easy to let go!" she remarked quite angrily, and another participant replied, "Well, you must be hanging on too tight!" How's that for wisdom?

If I have seen further, it is by standing on the shoulders of giants. — Isaac Newton.

Knowing Why Isn't Enough

It is one thing to find the wisdom from our pain; it is another thing altogether to use that wisdom to create a new way of living. Woody Allen once said, "I've spent thirty years in therapy, and I can tell you every disorder I have. I just don't know how to change them!"

It can be seductively easy to get caught up in the energy of the event rather than finding the core issues and changing the associated ineffective behaviors, thoughts, and/or attitudes.

Most of us can connect our past to *why* we are the way we are, yet we continue to replicate the same pattern of negativity. Discovering the *why* is just the first part of the journey. Most of us get to this stage and stop. We don't *do* anything with it. We don't continue into the challenging arena of changing the way we *do* our lives.

It's not enough to change just our perception of our painful memories. The only way for us to live a different life is to learn from what we have experienced and, more important, to take action—to change our behaviors in order to get a different result in the future. There's no easy way through it; we just have to do the work.

Let me give you an example. A man once told me that he had always felt ridiculed by one of his parents when growing up. This criticism was quite cruel and often presented in the presence of others. As a result, he had spent much of his childhood feeling insecure, with a low self-worth. Years later, he had grown into a very confident, self-assured adult with healthy self-esteem, but even with this empowerment, he continued to allow that parent to judge him, doing nothing to protect himself from the barrage of criticism.

Why? Because of—as he said—*fear*. He didn't take the affirmative action of having the tough conversation with this parent because he feared that it would be too uncomfortable—not just for the parent, but more so for himself.

We often live our lives in the guise of false humility. "I just didn't want to hurt their feelings" is an excuse that many of us have used to hide the fact that it was our own

fear that prevented us from being honest. I'm not saying that we have to be brutally frank, but those other people we claim to fear won't get the opportunity to modify
their behavior if they don't even know there's a problem in
the first place! As the wonderful saying goes, "If nothing
changes, nothing changes," and feedback can be one of the
greatest teachers of all.

Chapter 7

There Are No Failures in Life — Just Feedback

The title of this chapter is one of the most helpful phrases I have ever heard. Many of us go to the Pit when we receive feedback that we don't like. Throughout my many years of studying human behavior, I have found that the only time people really stretch themselves beyond their current level is when they receive feedback on what they're not doing right.

Professional Pit People don't know how to handle feedback. They interpret constructive criticism as a personal attack, which sends them spiraling deeper into their Pit. What kind of feedback do we like? Positive feedback, of course, such as "Gosh, you're gorgeous!" And what sort of feedback do we hate? We hate the negative stuff, such as "I wouldn't date you for practice!" Now, I'm being playful here, but there's truth at the core of this joke. As a society, we've become conditioned to want only the positive feedback. We tend to perceive anything negative as unhelpful, yet the reality is often quite the opposite.

Positive feedback *is* wonderful, and we all need to

become much more generous at giving positive feedback. However, positive feedback only reinforces what we already know about ourselves. It's only when we're shown the gaps that we're able to grow.

Let's say your business goes broke. Did you fail? No! You just got some feedback on how not to run a business next time!

Let's say you got the worst possible exam results. Did you fail? No, of course not! Again, you just got some feedback that you should have studied harder!

I'm being a bit playful here, and I know we're talking about serious topics. But it's true that we *never* fail. Life just gives us feedback on a regular basis. Adopting this outlook is a healthier and more empowering way to handle the results life serves us. Rather than shrinking into the pain of "failing," this is a way of perceiving the situation as an opportunity to grow.

If we perceive our results as failure instead of feedback, we can feel sorry for ourselves, and often we'll sink into our Pit. If we accept that every result we get in life is simply *feedback*, whether it's positive or negative, each situation will present us with a learning opportunity, and we'll stay out of the Pit.

Sometimes a negative result or certain events can bring on reactions like shock, sadness, grief, anger, despair, denial, humiliation, resentment, and so on. As I mentioned in chapter 5, feeling these emotions is important, and experiencing them is not the same as going into the Pit.

However, when we get *stuck* in these emotions and we don't move on, we are in danger of becoming a permanent Pit Person. We keep replaying the event as if it's happening again, over and over, so we run the risk of becoming habitually sad, resentful, angry, or whatever our emotional reaction may be. Looking at these experiences as nothing more than feedback frees us to move through the emotions so that we can find and learn the valuable lessons that come from the events and situations of our life.

If we don't perceive it as feedback, we can easily become consumed by our reaction. We can also become quite defensive when hearing feedback we don't like. It's not unusual for some people to "shoot the messenger"; they attack or persecute the person who has been courageous enough to speak up to help them grow. Have you ever asked someone for feedback and then wished you hadn't, because their comments were so accurate — and painful? I happen to have a great example.

It was a couple of years after my divorce, and I was feeling very positive about where we all were at in our life. The boys and I were settled in our new home, and we were happy, so I was doing a bit of contemplation. After watching an *Oprah* show in which a son commented on how his mother had just *loved* her life and this was the greatest lesson he had learned from her, I wondered what it was like for my children to have to hang out with me every day. So I thought I would ask Harison, who was twelve at the time.

Now, if you ask someone a question, make sure you've got enough honesty and courage to hear the answer! I said, "Honey, how would you describe Mommy? You know, how do you see me? If you had to say 'Mommy is . . . ,' what would you say?"

His reply was immediate: "Oh, sad."

I was shocked. "Sorry?" I questioned.

He repeated, with absolute confidence, "I see you as being sad."

I was stunned, because the last thing I felt was sad. So I proceeded to thank him for his honesty and explained that I thought it was interesting he perceived me as sad, as I was actually very happy. "What is it that I do that makes you think I'm sad, sweetheart?" I asked.

He replied so beautifully and clearly, "Oh, Mom, it's just that you keep going around saying how tired you are all the time. Like when you come home from work, you say how tired you are and how hard you work and that you travel all the time, so I just thought if you're working so hard and you're tired all the time, you must be sad."

How cool is that for feedback? I couldn't believe it. I reassured Harison that I was very happy with my life and that I wasn't tired or sad. I have my sad and tired moments, I explained, but I'm not sad and tired all the time. Harison was right—that was my tape that I had been playing for years—a tape I had learned from my mother. It was so unconscious I wasn't even aware of it until he mentioned it! Yes, I get tired, but I think we can get so addicted to these repetitive tapes that we don't stop to assess whether they're still appropriate. From that wonderful moment of exceptionally honest feedback, I was able to let go of a tired and worn-out tape that was no longer relevant.

How often do we continue with old habits and patterns from the past that no longer serve us? We tend not to question whether our responses and dialogue are appropriate anymore.

There's a wonderful story about a man who notices that

his wife cuts the ends off the ham before she bakes it. He asks, "Honey, why did you do that?"

"I do it because my mother always does it that way," she replies.

He decides to ask his mother-in-law the same question. "Mom, why do you cut the ends off the ham before you bake it?"

"I do it because my mother has always done it," she says.

So the husband goes to his grandmother-in-law and asks, "Grandma, why do you cut the ends off the ham before you bake it?"

"Oh, sweetheart, it's because my baking dish is too small!"

We all have opportunities to grow from feedback — if we're open to them. For example, I was working with someone at a recent event. He was a lovely person, very helpful, and eager to assist. At the same time, I noticed that nearly all of his communication had a negative tone, which became quite exhausting after a while, so I decided to share this with him. I explained that even though I found him personally to be very positive, his dialogue was quite negative; it was just the way he phrased things. He looked at me in shock and said quite harshly, "No one has ever, ever called me negative before!"

I said, *"You're* not negative; it's just your dialogue. I don't see you as negative at all, but your dialogue can be very much that way. You use terms like 'That won't work.' 'This can't happen.' 'They'll never say yes.' 'Don't do that.' I find it quite challenging to stay positive and upbeat when we're communicating."

Please understand, it was hard for me to say this to him — no one wants to say anything that might offend — but I was being affected by his negative dialogue. I waited for him to become defensive, but surprisingly, he appreciated and accepted my feedback. He just looked at me, and it was like *wow!* The penny had dropped.

What I loved most about him was that he didn't let his Pitman (also known as ego) get in the way of his growth. He stopped, paid attention to the feedback, and then was honest enough to take it on board as truth for him. Something obviously resonated, because in every communication we had after that, he made a conscious effort to use more empowering dialogue. He would start to say, "Don't —" but then catch himself and reword it in a positive frame. He took responsibility for his communication and welcomed feedback to enhance his life. What a great teacher he is for us all! I learned a lot from him and his reaction, and I hope you have too.

Bring It In!

Accepting feedback may seem easy as a concept, but when we're sensitive to the feedback, it can be challenging to welcome it in the moment. One evening, I decided to make my boys a new dish for dinner — tuna Mornay. I was assured by some of the moms at school that the boys would love it, and I proudly placed the new meal in front of them.

Harison took a mouthful and screwed up his face. He poked out his tongue and scraped off the tuna Mornay with the back of his knife. "This is disgusting!" he complained, with his tongue still poking out.

I said, "I just spent all afternoon preparing this for you, so don't be so ungrateful!"

Using his fingers as quotation marks, he replied, "It's just 'feedback,' Mom!" We all burst into laughter as I realized I had again received a *learning opportunity* about my son's tastes!

It's all in the delivery, isn't it? Respectful feedback means that we've stopped and thought about how the receiver of the feedback is going to take that information. We've considered the outcome that we want. If the outcome we want is wounded staff, or wounded partners, or wounded children, or wounded friends, then we can go ahead, fire those caustic bullets, and spray our anger and inability to control our tempers under the guise of "helping." We may not have great relationships in the end, but it's OK — we can use that lame excuse "I was just being honest." That's not honesty. That's brutal frankness, and it's cruel. If we stop for a moment and consider how to word our feedback, it will probably be better received. If we genuinely want to help the receivers, they will more than likely sense this. When people feel our true intention, our words may sting a little, but they will know that we had their best interests at heart.

How did you react the last time you received feedback from someone? Did you think about it much? Did you tell anyone about it? In the initial stages of receiving feedback, we tend to be too emotional to properly digest all the lessons.

Have you ever called someone close to you immediately after receiving feedback, in order to badger him or her into listening to your complaints about the "unfairness" of the feedback you received?

"You won't believe what Stacey said about me!"

"I was only ten minutes late for the meeting, and you should have heard him!"

"I'm only a day late with my assignment! What's her problem?"

"She's just jealous!"

Because we're in a hyperemotional state, the so-called "support" we receive after making such comments can be counterproductive. It can be difficult for us to be logical and to truly comprehend what's being said. We react by going into a self-protective mode.

One of the ways I handle feedback that really stings is to pretend that there is nothing and no one outside of me that I can blame for how I feel. This way, I can really "sit" in the situation and look at my part in it objectively. I "bring it in" and ask, "How did I contribute to this result? What was my part in it? What did I do or not do to create this? What is the lesson for me?" When I do this, I find my lessons so much faster, and the sting of the feedback is replaced with a gratitude for the new wisdom. Pitman, of course, hates this path, and he will be there all the while, coaxing us back to the Pit, where our sensibility is replaced with the highly charged reaction of revenge, blame, justification, or pity.

When we put everything outside of ourselves and make other people and situations responsible for how we feel, we completely give up the gift of self-awareness. Our greatest achievement and key to peace is to allow our feelings to come through — to rise within us, regardless of the pain, and to accept them with love — all of them, even the ones we may have been taught to judge. They are all clues to uncovering the mystery of "us." By owning all of our emotions we can look inside of ourselves, bring personal responsibility into our being, and ultimately completely own our life. When we learn to *bring it in*, we are then able to let our pain out, and the healing begins.

I also use this technique with my boys and with my team. We have all learned to bring it in when we find ourselves in that tempting place of making someone or something else responsible for our situation and our feelings. It would be great if we could immediately go to this reflective place, but sometimes our highly charged reaction needs time to dissipate. Only when we have time to calm down are we able to bring it in and see the powerful learning opportunities available to us from the experience. We can then begin to accept a part of us that we may have denied. That's why it is so powerful to create a gap between the stimulus and the response we give it — the bigger the gap, the more rational we're likely to be.

If you want to get maximum benefit from the feedback you receive, simply follow these two key steps:

Step 1.   *Say "Thank you."* Be appreciative of the fact that someone cared enough about you to put the heat on, to help you grow.

Step 2.   *Wait twenty-four to forty-eight hours* before discussing the feedback with anyone (especially with someone you care about). This will allow ample time for your emotions to settle and enable you to objectively take the feedback on board. If, after this time, you still think the person was being totally unfair, at least you've had time to digest the input objectively.

So the next time you receive feedback, remember to smile and say, "Thank you." Then wait twenty-four hours and bring it in.

Chapter 8

Happiness Is a Choice

How we deal with feedback is really about choice. Whether we interpret the feedback positively or negatively depends on the perception we choose to adopt. It can be tempting to make it about the other person or the circumstance. But whether we see it as a personal attack or an opportunity for growth is our choice.

A woman who worked for me years ago was constantly late, especially for work, and when I would question her about it, she would blame the bus! "The bus is always late!" she would exclaim, not realizing that it wasn't the bus's responsibility to get her to work on time. It was her responsibility. My suggestion that she catch an earlier bus was not received with much gratitude — and she would continue to not be grateful for it until she took ownership of her punctuality. Taking personal responsibility and blaming others can rarely coexist.

But what about all of the other factors that influence our day-to-day moods? How do we go about staying optimistic? When we feel down, rarely does anyone show us *how* to get out of the Pit. It's a bit like the advice given by well-meaning people who say things like, "Don't take your personal problems to work. Make sure you leave them at the front door." But has anyone ever shown us how to *not* take our personal problems to work? And what about the line, "Don't take this personally," which invariably precedes personal criticism and is usually followed by the word "but"?

One of my friends was laid off from her job. As she was handed the termination letter, her manager said, "Now don't take this personally." She replied sarcastically, "I find it very hard not to—the letter starts with 'Dear Carol'!"

Wouldn't it be empowering to be able to deal with life's ups and downs in an optimistic and objective way? Wouldn't it be wonderful if we had a formula to avoid taking our personal problems to work? What if we had a process that enabled us to jump out of that Pit whenever we wanted to? Our lives would improve dramatically if we were fully empowered to make that choice. If only we had a process whereby we didn't need an outside influence in order for us to *feel* or *act* in a healthy, positive way again. Would you like to know a process that could enable you to change from being a Pit dweller to living a life full of energy and optimism? Would that be of benefit to you?

A lot of us would like to live our lives out of the Pit, but being a victim has its advantages too! It gives us an out, often providing an opportunity for us to blame others for our problems, as well as offering an excuse for why our life isn't working. To some of us, the fear of walking through our pain seems too great, so under the guise of "they did it to me" we settle for a lesser, more numb life.

The difficult news for really serious Pit dwellers is that when they learn how to live outside of the Pit, they can no longer blame others for their problems. That's probably why the Professional Pit People don't want exposure to this type of information.

To live outside of the Pit, you must accept that *you* are *personally* responsible for your own life; it is *you* who place yourself in the Pit, and *you* are the only one who can get yourself out. It's like a self-renovation—but you're the only one on the site! This is one task you can't delegate. Sure, you can reflect, get advice, read books, and attend self-improvement courses—but at the end of the day, *it is you alone who can change you.*

You have to be the person who takes positive action. No lover, no weight-loss program, no job, no house, no child, no school result, no company profit, no friend, and no amount of money will get you out of that Pit if you're not willing to climb that ladder yourself. Will your support group be waiting for you at the top? Who knows? But you have a much better chance of attracting positive support into your life if you have a positive projection.

To be positive in your outlook, you don't need to be yee-ha!-ing all over the place. I sometimes cringe when I hear people saying things like, "Positive! Positive! Positive! We've just gotta be positive!" When I use the word "positive," I'm not talking about being a constant cheerleader, seeing the world through rose-colored glasses, or being blindly optimistic. Being positive simply means taking life as it comes and being present in all of the situations life offers. Positive people have certain things in common:

- They sometimes spend time alone in reflection.

- They give themselves permission to experience the entire range of their emotions, including sadness, excitement, grief, joy, anger, despair, disappointment, and happiness. They realize that's a positive thing to do.

- They use their limitations to their advantage and to the benefit of others.

Some of the most positive people I've ever met have been quiet, deep thinkers who in their so-called darkest moments have created some of the most amazing outcomes. On the other hand, some of us think both the answer and the problem are outside of ourselves. We can waste a lot of time and energy waiting for that magical person to come along or event to occur to save us. The magical answer we've been looking for has been within us all along. So if you're ready to live a life outside of the Pit, then keep reading.

Take Ownership

On the following pages you will find a few simple strategies to support you in living a life that allows you to operate from ownership, not blame. Living a life of ownership means we accept how we react to a situation or event. We can't always be responsible for what life throws at us, but we *can* always be responsible for how we react to any situation, even the most traumatic ones.

In contrast, operating in a blame state (becoming a Pitman) finds us consistently placing the responsibility for how we feel outside of ourselves. I am not saying that we will never go to the Pit again. Of course we will. We all will. It's just that after learning the next stage, you'll determine how long you stay there. One of the greatest freedoms I have is knowing that I am 100 percent responsible for how I feel. Do I still feel frustrated and angered by the actions of others? Of course! But I know that I choose my reactions every single time. When we realize this, we start to exercise this emotional muscle, and it becomes easier to notice when and who we give our power away to, especially when we're upset or reactionary.

Ownership: "I still go to the Pit occasionally, and every time I'm in there, I know it was *me* who put me there, nobody else. I am not responsible for how others behave, but I am responsible for how I interpret that behavior and how I react to it."

Blame: "I would have done, been, had . . . if it had not been for . . ." Most of us have existed in a state of blame at certain points in our lives. There are phrases that can warn us when we're in a "blame" state:

"They did it to me!"

"It's not my fault I'm like this."

"If only you hadn't . . ."

"Why is this happening to me?"

"It's not fair!"

"How was I supposed to know?"

"Nothing I do is ever good enough."

"I can't believe he treated me like that!"

"Nothing ever goes right for me."

How often do we hear friends or partners blame each other for their behavior?

"Why did you let me drink so much?"

"Why didn't you tell me I had spent so much?"

"If you hadn't done that, then I wouldn't have done this!"

"How could you let me embarrass myself like that?"

"Why didn't you stop me?"

"How could you upset me by behaving like that?"

"If only you hadn't done that to me!"

"Can you imagine what other people thought when you did that?"

This kind of talk doesn't serve anyone's higher good. So how can we operate from a position that takes full responsibility for how we show up in the world? We are personally responsible for how we experience the world through our thought processes. When we take responsibility for our personal perception, we can stop blaming others for how we feel.

Let me share with you a fun anecdote about the power

of perception. We use this great example when doing customer-service training.

An aggressive guy walks up to the check-in counter at an international airport. In a loud, gruff voice, he says to the check-in clerk, "Jack Byrne—Toronto!" and throws his passport onto the counter, indifferent to the fact that it hits the young woman's hand. As the clerk checks the screen, she cringes. Mr. Byrne's flight closed fifteen minutes ago, and she isn't looking forward to delivering the bad news. She looks up at Mr. Byrne, who is impatiently tapping his fingers on the counter, and says in a most apologetic voice, "I am so sorry, sir. That flight is now closed, and unfortunately—"

Not letting her complete her sentence, he bursts into a tirade of abuse. "What do you mean the flight is closed? Reopen it! Call the plane immediately. Let them know I've arrived!"

The clerk tries to pacify Mr. Byrne with empathy. "Sir, I can imagine your frustration and how inconvenient this is for you. It's just that—"

She is again interrupted by another blast. "Don't give me that! Do you know who I am? Who do you think you are, you blonde bimbo! I'm going to have your job for this—just you wait!"

The clerk explains that she has put him on the next flight, and as she tags his bags, she can feel his wrath as he huffs and puffs. She hands him his boarding pass. Snatching it from her hand, he yells, "This isn't the last you've heard from me!"

He storms off, leaving the clerk standing there to receive

her next passenger. "Good afternoon, sir," she says in a calm, professional manner and with a big smile. "Thank you for your patience."

The next passenger cannot believe the clerk's amazing ability to handle such an abusive outburst and then instantly switch her headspace to being emotionally ready to receive the next passenger. He can't praise her enough. "I just have to say that I've never seen anyone handle such an aggressive person in such a calm and empathic way. You're amazing! How do you do it?"

"Well," she says with a cheeky smile, "I have a special way of dealing with people like that."

"Oh, do tell!"

"All I can say is that I would love to be in Toronto to see Mr. Byrne's face when he finds out that his luggage has gone to Tokyo!"

They both burst out laughing. Then the clerk admits she's only kidding. "But it is an enticing thought. We all have bad days, and although I was a little shaken by his rudeness, I accept that it wasn't really about me. Maybe he doesn't know how to handle situations like that, or maybe he's had a really rough day. Two wrongs don't make a right, and revenge has never opened the door to compassion and understanding."

This clerk could have blamed Mr. Byrne for upsetting her. She also could have taken her feelings out on other customers. She could have stayed in a bad mood for the rest of the day. She could have let it affect her confidence as well. But she didn't do any of these things, and this had nothing to do with anybody but her! She took responsibility for how she perceived the situation, and as a result, she was in control of her reaction and her emotions.

I see the two approaches—ownership and blame—as similar to different roles in the making of a movie. Taking ownership means you are the director, creating the story; casting blame means you are simply an actor in the movie, playing out the role under someone else's direction and control. Remember, your life is *your* movie. You get the chance to reinterpret the scenes and create a new meaning for any experience you have encountered. When we start to see every situation and event in our life as an opportunity for our evolution or enlightenment, we don't waste valuable time and energy feeling sorry for ourselves. We give ourselves that most valuable gift of choice!

I believe one of the greatest ownership teachers on the planet is Nelson Mandela. The story goes that when Nelson Mandela was in prison, he would give thanks to the guards for punishing him. If he had to carry boulders all day, he would thank the prison guards for giving him a task that would strengthen his muscles and keep him fit. If he was sent to solitary confinement, he would give thanks for the space and solitude to clear his thoughts and strengthen his clarity. Everything that was thrown at him, he chose to receive with gratitude. What a powerful lesson for us all. The next time you face a challenge, rather than feeling defeated, find the gift! Nelson Mandela had every reason to live in the Pit while in prison, but he chose to perceive his incarceration differently, and in so doing he inspired a world by his courage.

So how can I get out of the Pit?

Chapter 9

Perception

We now know enough to be able to recognize when we are using Pit behavior and language — or when someone else is. I'm also hoping that by now we recognize how debilitating it can be. Whether we're a few inches deep or all the way down in the basement, knowing how to get out of the Pit is essential. Realizing we have the choice allows us to decide on the kind of life we want to live. It doesn't matter how much money we have, how many possessions we have, what level of education we've reached, how many friends we enjoy, what job we hold, what has happened in our past, or what we look like!

> No one can go back and make a brand-new
> start, my friend, but anyone can start from here
> and make a brand-new end.
>
> — ATTRIBUTED TO MARCUS AURELIUS, CARL BRAND,
> DAN ZADRA, AND OTHERS

In modern psychology it's often said that a person's past behavior is a strong indicator of his or her future behavior.

There's an important distinction to be made: the future is *not* written in stone. Just because we behaved a certain way in our past does not mean we *have* to be that way in the future.

Our past ways of thinking and behaving can certainly influence us, but we must become the guardians of our thoughts and behaviors — of how we judge others and ourselves. Our earlier discussions on being dissociated and associated can support us in perceiving everything as an opportunity to grow. Judgment kills growth and never allows for a greater expansion of our current knowledge.

Perception and the Pit

Remember that house with the four different-colored sides viewed by four different people? They all agreed it was a house, but each person saw it as a different-colored house. And reality is the same; depending on our view of it, our experience of it will be different from others'. How we *perceive* something — a situation, an event, or a person — will ultimately determine how we feel, and this feeling then affects how we project ourselves. It's the same when two people experience the same event and have completely

Hmm . . . how can I
get out of the Pit?

different perceptions of it. Why? Because there is no such thing as pure perception. Our perception of the world is influenced by many factors, such as our upbringing, values, culture, beliefs, education, temperament, experiences, and age.

Many of us can also make the mistake of creating a global opinion of a local event. Take, for example, relationships. Some of us may have had a string of "bad" relationships, and instead of taking responsibility for our part in attracting and maintaining such a relationship (local), we make our experience global (for example, "All men/women are #&*%#!"). We then project this global perception onto all of our future relationships. It's almost as if we go in expecting to get the same result as we did in our past relationships. If you had a relationship with a partner who cheated on you, and you've made this a global perception, you may perceive everyone as untrustworthy, waiting to take advantage of you and hurt you. You might then act with a mistrusting, cynical, and guarded attitude. Whether we share such an assumption with others or even just continually think about it, we strengthen it, and therein lies our self-fulfilling prophecy. What we think about, we attract and create!

On the other hand, if you perceive yourself as a confident, loving, and enthusiastic person, you will be more likely to project a confident, loving, and enthusiastic persona, and again, you will strengthen this thought process. Life is a mirror. If we see an ugly, negative world, how do we think the world responds? When we have the courage to *not* share our negative thoughts, we weaken them. That's why gossip is so highly charged; the more we gossip, the more it's fuelled.

It's the same with every situation and event in our lives. Every day, we have a choice as to how to perceive what we experience.

I have a story from my childhood that typifies this beautifully for me. When I was about four or five years old, I had a big wart on my right knee, and to my young eyes, it looked huge!

It didn't bother me that much until one day I fell down the stairs at home and it came off in the fall. There was blood everywhere, so my mother threw me a towel and told me to clean up the mess. She was a nurse, and my five siblings and I rarely got much sympathy for what she called "minor flesh wounds." I can still fondly recall my mother saying, "You think that's a wound? Come to the hospital, and I'll show you a wound!" We certainly grew up as a resilient bunch!

Well, my small wound healed, and that was the end of it—or so I thought. Over the following years, warts started to appear and multiply all over my body. By the time I was ten years old, I had warts all over my legs and toes. I had plantar warts on the soles of my feet, and I had large, unsightly warts on my fingers and arms. In fact, the entire end of my right index finger was a wart, which prevented the nail from growing properly. They were everywhere; I even had them on my face.

It was so revolting for me, and I felt like the ugliest person alive. This wasn't just a momentary feeling. It was a feeling that was with me practically all day, every day. I was continually counting my warts. The highest number I ever got to was 167, and they stayed around that number for many years. The warts persisted right through that totally self-conscious and insecure stage called puberty. When I was about twelve or thirteen, I was sitting beside a boy at school who also had a lot of warts on his feet. I remember thinking how disgusting they looked, and that's when it dawned on me how disgusting I must look to other people. I felt like I was a living, breathing, walking, talking wart, and that was all I was—a wart. That feeling continued through those painful teenage years. I remember being about fifteen and feeling so sorry for myself. I couldn't believe how unfair life was to me. I constantly wondered what I had done to deserve such a cruel fate. My mother tried every old folk remedy she could think of to get rid of them. We tried all sorts of crazy things, but nothing ever worked. I would go to the doctor and endure the pain of having them frozen off, but the results were always the same: nothing ever changed, and they just grew back with a vengeance. I was desperate to get rid of those warts, and my whole life revolved around how ugly I felt because of them.

Looking back, I had many profound learning opportunities because of my warts. One of those opportunities came about in my mid-teens when I had just started dating one of the cutest boys in town. Apart from the fact that I was in shock that he had asked me out, I was also convinced that once he saw my warts, he would not want to go out with me again. I resigned myself to just enjoying it while it lasted. One afternoon, we were sitting together at the park, and he began affectionately rubbing the outside of my lower right leg. This was where the majority of the warts had clustered. It was like slow motion. As he got closer to the "wart zone," I froze. His hand reached the warts, and I felt like dying. But then a strange and wonderful thing happened. He paused for a microsecond, and I thought, *Great, he just touched the freak's warts. He's going to scream and run away.* But he didn't. He continued his affectionate display, and I started to feel amazing. In that moment, I had my first glimpse of what it felt like to be completely accepted regardless of what I looked like. I will never forget him for showing me, for just a moment, that I was more than my warts.

About two years after that, my brother was involved in a serious motorbike accident and was placed on life support. I remember walking into the intensive care unit and seeing him with perfect skin. He had had mild acne when he was admitted, but now his face was as smooth as a baby's bottom. It was only for a split second, but I remember thinking *If I were on life support, then maybe my warts would go too!*

It was a crazy thought, I know. But that's when I got a flash of sudden awareness and understanding, something often referred to as *satori*. It's that sensation we have all had: one moment we don't know, and the very next, we do! I remember thinking, *You idiot. Your brother's fighting for his life, and you're complaining about a few lumps and bumps on your body.* It was a defining moment for me. At seventeen years old, I made a decision. I decided that I wasn't my warts. I realized that I had two arms and two legs, I had an OK body, an OK personality, and I was reasonably attractive. I also knew that I could tell a good joke and make people laugh — something I loved doing. I accepted that I had a lot going for me, and I decided that rather than being consumed with my (perceived) ugliness, as I had been for many years, I was going to be grateful for what I had. I was not going to focus on those warts anymore. I started to own my life.

I don't know exactly when it happened, but about six or seven months later, as I was climbing out of bed, I looked at my legs and noticed there were white dots where the warts had been. Every single wart was gone!

In that moment I felt a joy that I had never felt before. What a wonderful metaphor for life, for all of us who hang on to something that we think defines us. I had been blaming my warts for the fact that I didn't feel that I was good enough. I blamed them for my not feeling attractive, for not being invited to parties, and so they had become the reason I couldn't do this or that. Whatever it was, I blamed my warts.

We all have a "wart story," don't we? Something that we think defines us. Something that we think will stop other people from loving us, from accepting us "warts and all."

But we are not our past. We are not the events that have happened to us. We are so much more than that! So rather than judge ourselves, let's celebrate the beautiful tapestry that we have become *because* of all these colorful threads, not in spite of them.

To finish my wart story, many years later, when Jackson was about two and a half, he started to get small lumps on his neck. They looked like baby warts to me, and I was filled with dread. His little friend had them as well, and his mother would squeeze the core out to make them go away. I was filled with horror that my own son would be facing a tortured childhood like mine, so I suggested to him that we, too, do this "procedure." He looked at me with absolute shock on his face, put his little chubby hands around his neck, and said loudly, "No, Mama! I lub my lumps!"

I laughed and hugged him tight. Jackson's lumps disappeared by themselves a few weeks later. My wonderful toddler had taught me that self-love is one of the greatest gifts we can have. He taught me to "lub" all my bits!

Judgment Is Also a Perception

Another way in which perception works in our lives is through judgment. Self-judgment and judgment of others is a Pitman way of living. It amazes me how easily, how quickly and harshly we can judge others and ourselves. Many years ago, someone asked whether I felt judged by my audiences during my presentations. I had to laugh. "Judge me?" I said. "They start at my shoes and work their way up!"

"Does it worry you?" was the next question.

"No. It used to bother me, but now my self-esteem is a lot healthier. It was my insecurity that made me so sensitive to other people's perception of me, but those feelings taught me a great deal. I realized that I am not my hair, and I am not my clothes. I am not my shoes, and I am not my age. I am not my skin, and I am not my gender. The outside of me is what I like to call my wrapping paper. The outside is just how life happened to wrap me up. Terry Hawkins is on the inside."

We all have different wrapping paper. Even identical twins are wrapped with slightly different wrapping paper. One of the saddest things I've come to realize over the years is that if we don't like a person's wrapping paper, we don't necessarily bother to find the gift inside. I came up with that analogy after watching a television commercial for people living with blindness. A couple was getting married. *How sad*, I thought. *They'll never have the opportunity to see each other.* Then I got another *satori*! How wonderful that they were marrying for the right reasons—for *who* they were and not what they looked like! That's when I had my epiphany about racism. If we were all born blind, it would be difficult for racism to exist. Racism is actually illogical—think about that for a moment. If we couldn't see the color of someone's skin, then we wouldn't be able to judge them for that. I believe that when we judge another person, for whatever reason, we're saying a lot more about ourselves than we are about them.

I find that I judge others when I'm feeling insecure. Pay attention the next time you make someone wrong simply because that person lives his or her life differently than you live yours. That's what judgment is to me—making another person wrong simply because he or she has chosen a different path. Why are some of us so frightened to let others be different? Just as other people are not their wrapping paper, neither are you. There is so much more to all of us than what is on the outside. So don't stay in the Pit just because you believe that someone gave you a good reason to be there. Remember, it's all *perception*.

I know that sometimes in life it can feel as though we're locked up in chains. For each of us, though, there comes a time when we need to find our key and unlock the things that inhibit us — unlock our old way of operating, and create a new, more empowered way of life. And this is where Flipman enters the building.

Chapter 10

Mind Mechanics

We have talked a lot about the way we perceive the world and how it influences our reality. In order for us to take control of our life and the results we produce, it might be important to first look at the mechanics of how this actually happens.

Let's begin by having a look at the three parts of this process—the conscious mind, the unconscious (or subconscious) mind, and our physiology. I have often heard the conscious mind described as the captain of our brain. It gives directions and tells the unconscious mind what to do. The unconscious mind becomes the crew. The crew doesn't think for itself—it just does what it's told. Our physiology is thus profoundly shaped by our conscious and unconscious mind.

Mind Language

Captain: We make a perception or interpret an experience.

Crew: The unconscious mind accepts this interpretation.

Outcome: The body then aligns itself with this input.

Let's go into a bit more detail.

Captain

The first stage is about how we perceive the world. We chat inside our head all the time. Chat, chat, and more chat. Most of us are completely oblivious to the conversations, interpretations, and perceptions that go on between our ears. If we are to take control of how we react and behave, we must listen to this internal voice.

What are you telling yourself right now? You may be saying, "This is really interesting. I've never looked at it that way before." Or you may be saying, "This is so confusing!" Whatever we say inside will determine what happens for us outside. As we've discussed earlier, *our perception creates our reality*. How we perceive anything determines our reaction to it, emotionally, physically, and biologically. The biggest challenge is that most of us don't own the talk that goes on inside our heads. We can easily talk in a way that disempowers us, and those around us, and not even be aware of it. A common example of this is when we make someone or something else responsible for how we feel. For example, "Public speaking makes me terrified!" It isn't the public speaking that makes us terrified, it's our perception of public speaking that creates these debilitating feelings. When we own our perceptions and thoughts, we can then consider how to reframe our perception so that it has a less hindering effect on us.

Crew

In the second stage, our unconscious mind accepts this perception as truth.

Our unconscious mind instantly accepts whatever we tell ourselves, because our unconscious mind doesn't know the difference between fact and fiction. This is why it's crucial to pay attention to the actual language and dialogue we use. Take, for example, relationships. It's easy to criticize and complain about our partners, but just think how damaging it is to the relationship when one or both parties think that sarcastic quips are a form of humor. Sarcasm requires making a joke at someone else's expense. And even after the "Sorry—only joking, honey" has come and gone, the damage has been done. That moment has been recorded in the unconscious mind. Twenty years into a relationship, we may be surprised to hear a couple say, "I don't know why, we just don't seem to love each other anymore." Yet their unconscious minds are screaming, "I know the reason! It's because we keep saying all of those horrible things to each other, and we believe them!" And then we wonder why we fall out of love.

Right after the unconscious mind receives a message, the third stage occurs.

Outcome

In the third stage, the body aligns itself to the unconscious mind. Whatever perception we register, the unconscious mind accepts, and in turn the body just follows, aligning itself.

Let's put all this together:

a) **Captain**—conscious mind
Perception: You tell yourself there is a monster in the cupboard.

b) **Crew**—unconscious mind
Interpretation: The unconscious mind then accepts this as truth. It says, "Well, you know far better than I do, so I believe you," at which point it sends a message directly to the body, and then . . .

c) **Outcome**—physiology
Alignment: The body aligns itself to the unconscious mind and the perception. It creates a biological response that produces chemicals to make you feel terrified.

This process occurs in many areas of our lives and can wreak havoc. Here's an example that I'm sure a lot of couples can relate to. At a large social gathering, you see your partner speaking to a very attractive person. You happen to be feeling insecure about yourself of late, and in that moment *you form a perception* that your partner is flirting. If you apply the process, what emotions might you experience in your body? Jealousy, rage, sadness? These emotions are a result of your *perception* of the situation, not of *the situation itself*. A few moments later, you discover that the attractive person is your partner's cousin, and almost instantly your emotions change because now you have a different perception.

Candace Pert, Ph.D., a celebrated molecular biologist and psychoneuroimmunologist and author of *Molecules of*

Emotion: The Science Behind Mind-Body Medicine, discovered
that the existence of peptides and their receptors demonstrates how the mind and body communicate: we actually
have biochemical reactions to mental and emotional stimuli — our everyday thoughts and feelings. After decades of
research, Dr. Pert finally made clear how emotion creates
the bridge between mind and body and has coined a term
for it: "bodymind."

To really simplify it, our emotions are a chemical reactions to a thought — to our perceptions — so that everything we feel emotionally we have actually created. How we
feel then affects how we interpret the world, and we create
either Flipman energy or Pitman energy.

Chapter 11

Fake It Till You Make It!

My aim in creating Flipman and Flipman's Strategy was to have a simple, powerful analogy that we could all integrate into our daily lives—a character and concept that could represent choice in every moment and support us in creating the life we really want, regardless of our background, our religious or spiritual beliefs, our educational level, our values or beliefs, our gender, our financial status, or our age. The concept of Flipman's Strategy actually began in my life many years ago; I just didn't recognize who he was then, and I hadn't named him yet. To give you a solid understanding of how we can use this simple yet powerful strategy, I would like to unfold this part for you in the same way that it evolved for me.

I begin with a short story from my early childhood. It illustrates how every day we have opportunities to learn from the amazing teachers around us, but we can recognize them only if we are paying attention.

One day when I was about eight years old, I was in a bad

mood with a grumpy expression on my face. My father said to me, "Terry, put a smile on your face."

I replied, "Well, then I'd be lying."

Dad said, "Sweetheart, I would much prefer one of your fake smiles to one of your sincere frowns!"

Well, of course, when you're eight, you think, "What an idiot!" But as I got older, I realized that my father was expressing, in his own words, that wonderful adage I'm sure you've heard a thousand times:

Fake it till you make it.

This is a great piece of advice, but how many of us realize just how powerful and life-changing its meaning can be? I spent many years wondering what this simple but often misunderstood saying really meant. I kept asking myself, "*How* do we 'fake it till we make it'?"

As I got older, my passion for finding the answer grew and grew. My desire to fully understand this concept and then be able to show people how to "fake it till you make it" became Flipman's Strategy. I asked myself: "What would I have to do to fake it till I made it? And how could I teach someone else to do the same?"

Over many years and in many training rooms, by answering those questions and then combining the answers with everything I had learned about the power of the brain, our mind, and our behavior, I formulated the Flipman character. It fueled my passion as a results-based trainer and educator to be able to help people *do* (the action), not just *know* (the theory). That way, they would eventually *be* (integration) whatever they wanted.

It was the *feeling*, the *doing*, and the *being* that became so powerful for me, along with answering the question, "Do you have to *feel* a certain way in order to *do* the behavior?" The answer: No, you don't! I wanted to show people that how they felt did not have to be the reason they couldn't change. I wanted to show people *how* to avoid affecting their work life with their personal issues, *how* to avoid taking things personally, *how* to avoid letting their past ruin their future, and *how* to take ownership of their life. I didn't want false hype and short-lived motivation. I wanted to offer people a solution—a strategy for staying out of the Pit.

I remember people reciting affirmations during the 1980s. In those days, people thought that all it would take for them to change would be regular recitations of a few positive phrases every day, such as, "I'm a powerful, positive, successful human being." The problem was, many of them had Pitman posture, Pitman projection, and Pitman thinking! More recently, many people have been seduced into thinking that all they have to do is visualize what they want and it will be theirs. Sure, thinking in a positive manner is certainly better than being in the Pit, but just thinking something is not going to make it manifest. My mother used to say that the only time *success* comes before *work* is in the dictionary! That's still true today. We have to actively participate in our own evolution.

So "fake it till you make it" took on a whole new meaning for me. It seemed to me that if we decide the outcomes we want and then act as if (fake it) we have already achieved them, then our unconscious mind won't know we are pretending. If we persevere in this, over time our mind and our body will align and we will grow new neural pathways to support our new way of being. I also know the word "fake" can be seen as negative. "I don't want to be fake!" Of course we don't want to be fake, and we're not being fake. I believe the word "fake," in this context, is to imitate. We imitate the positive thoughts, feelings, and behaviors that will support us.

As I've mentioned, in pondering the concept of "fake it till you make it" I also started asking myself, "How could I show someone how to do 'fake it till you make it'? What would that involve?" The answer may sound simple, but to be able to execute it to achieve the results we want, we need to fully understand the depth behind the simplicity. To be able to fake it till you make it, we need to *fake the positive behaviors, thoughts, and feelings that are opposite to the negative ones we're currently experiencing.*

Now, let's not rush this; it may sound simple, but as I said, it has many levels. So often we rush over what we *think* we know. If you want to really understand this, you need to go deeper. Let yourself sit in the knowledge for a while. Be with it. It's so easy to intellectualize knowledge without actually integrating it fully. I know for myself that I need to keep coming back to this process, especially when I occasionally allow myself to fall into the Pit. So let me repeat: If we are to fake it till we make it, we need to *fake the positive behaviors, thoughts, and feelings that are opposite to the negative ones we're currently experiencing.*

A journalist from *The Australian* interviewed me a few years back. He asked, "If you were to tell someone in one sentence how to feel motivated, what would you say?"

"Therein lies the problem!" I replied. "I aim to run two miles every day. Do you think that I wake up every day going, 'Yay! Woohoo! I'm going for a two-mile run!' No way! Especially on those really cold days, I fight with my Pitman. Sometimes he comes with me, all the way to the treadmill. 'Only do one mile today,' he teases with his seductive voice. Then I get a stitch in my side. 'Could be a tumor!' Pitman whispers, trying to seduce me off the treadmill."

The journalist laughed, and I explained further: "Have you ever seen the difference between people walking into the gym and the ones walking out? You can hear Handel's "Death March" playing on the way in and "Zip-A-Dee-Doo-Dah" on the way out. We let how we *feel* get in the way of what we *do*! People think they need to be *feeling* motivated to *do* motivated. We think we need to have the feeling first, in order to do the behavior, but we don't. It's usually the opposite. If we just make the decision, do the behavior, and fake the feeling for a while, more often than not we will actually start feeling it for real!"

This journalist was so moved by this simple but inspiring explanation that he decided to write a whole section on the topic!

Think about any part of our lives, from our relationships to mowing the lawn. When we don't overanalyze how we actually feel about it and "just do it," it's amazing how enjoyable it can be. More often than not, our feelings will eventually catch up with our behaviors. So instead of waiting for the feeling to arrive, why not behave that way first and pretend to feel it too? You'll soon find that you actually do start feeling that way. Instead of being stuck, you start moving.

We often don't move from where we are because we spend most of our time dreaming about where we want to *be*, and resenting where we are, without *doing* anything differently. "I want to *be* happy. I want to *be* fit. I want to *be* kind. I want to *be* wealthy." It's great to have goals, but goals are just the outcomes of *doing* the right behaviors, thoughts, and feelings. Change the word "be" to "do"—*do* happy, *do* kind, *do* wealthy, *do* fit—and you'll start to manifest the behaviors required to achieve these states. That's when you'll *be*. Doing is the bridge to being—going from conscious to unconscious.

Let me give you a quick example of how, by simply changing our behavior, we can change how we feel. Remember the grumpy look on my face that caught my dad's attention? How would you teach me to fake the positive behavior that's the opposite of feeling grumpy? What would you get me to *do*? Most people say, "Just smile and think happy thoughts" (I have a friend who can think the happiest thoughts ever, yet she still *looks* sad!).

When we say, "Smile," we're asking the person to *do* an *outcome*, and people can't *do* outcomes; we can only *do behaviors*. Smiling is the *outcome* from *doing* a series of behaviors that create the smile. We don't *do* a smile; we *get* a smile. We smile so habitually that we don't give a second thought to *how* we smile. Give yourself the time to really contemplate this important distinction, because when we can break down the habitual behaviors we do that create our current outcomes, we are far more able to create new behaviors that support the outcomes we most desire. This is where most of us get stuck. We don't even notice the habits we have that keep us stuck.

Think about the physical behaviors we need to *do* to change our faces from looking grumpy to looking happy (the opposite positive behavior) so that the outcome is a smile. Most of us will just start smiling without stopping to understand what we had to *do* to create that smile. Now as you smile, think about what your face is doing. Which way is it moving? What's happening with your eyes, your head, and your mouth?

Imagine a sad face. What behaviors would you need to *do* to that face to make it smile? Let's start with your head. How would it be positioned if you were grumpy?

Answer: Usually downcast. So the first opposite behavior could be to . . .

Lift up your head;

Open your eyes;

Lift the corners of your mouth;

. . . and finally,

Show your teeth.

Do all of those things, and you will end up with a happy face!

I can hear Pitman saying, "That's fine. I may be smiling, but I don't *feel* happy." The wonderful thing about all of this is, if we fake looking happy for a while, we will actually start to *feel* happy.

Can it be that simple? Yes, it can! Of course, if we want

to sustain these new behaviors there's a lot more to it, but we have to start somewhere. I'm not saying that this simple exercise is going to eradicate deep issues that need to be worked through, but it will help us operate in a state that supports us while we work through these very issues.

Play a game for me. Take your index finger and place it horizontally in your mouth, between your teeth, and push it back. (Yes, you will need to open your mouth.) Go on, no one's watching!

The moment you did that, the corners of your mouth went up because the zygomaticus (major cheek muscle) contracted or were pulled upwards. The brain recognized this behavior as the one you do when you're happy, so it started producing "feel good" chemicals. Studies show that endorphins, natural painkillers, and serotonin are released when we smile. All together these make us feel good.

Wouldn't you love to say to some Pit people in your life, "Shove a finger in your mouth and get happy"?

The three stages—conscious mind, unconscious mind, and physiology—show, in a very simplistic way, what we have discussed: how our brain processes our perceptions of our experiences, creating a biological response in our body. Therefore, if we make a conscious choice to change the way we perceive a situation or event and then support this perception with matching feelings and behaviors, we will be much more capable of creating the outcomes we're looking for. We need to become conscious of implementing the most effective internal and external strategy possible. We need a strategy to support the production of new neural pathways that are in line with the life we desire. That's where Flipman's Strategy comes in!

Chapter 12

Flipman's Strategy

Flipman's Strategy is a simple four-step process that encompasses the pictures, dialogue, feelings, and actions needed to help us replace old habits that don't serve us anymore with more empowering and positive habits. Flipman's Strategy will also support us in doing what is necessary to create these new habits and new neural pathways. Instead of just remembering to fake it, we can rely on a system to give us consistency and support when we need it most.

To explain this strategy, let's use the simple example of feeling tired. Like many expressions that don't serve us, "Gee, I'm tired" may seem like a throwaway line, but it can have a very negative effect on our energy, especially when there isn't time for a nap. Naturally, tiredness can be genuine and an important signal that we need a self-caring response: to sleep! But if we are at work or somewhere where we need to be alert, constantly saying we are tired does not serve us. Remember, whatever our conscious mind says, our unconscious mind believes and our body responds. So what do we need to ask ourselves? That is, "What positive behaviors, thoughts, and feelings are the opposite of tiredness?"

Alive! Awake! Energized!

In that moment, do we really feel alive, awake, and energized? Emphatically not! Does our unconscious mind know that? No—because it believes everything that we tell it. Remember that. In the initial stages of developing Flipman, I thought all I needed to do was go around telling myself, "I'm awake, I'm alive, I'm a happenin' girl!" But nothing happened! Nothing happened because I wasn't *doing* anything different; I hadn't changed any behaviors. I wasn't *faking* any actions till I *made it*. I was simply reciting a dialogue. I realized I needed to support the dialogue with a visual, auditory, kinesthetic, and "take-action" supporting stimulus. This became Flipman's Strategy.

As I mentioned in chapter 2, one of the most powerful aha! moments that I've ever had was realizing that if we know how to do Pitman, then we know how to do Flipman. Creating negative outcomes still requires us to *see, say, feel,* and *do* the negatives. Think about it: when we're in the Pit, we continually think about how bad our life is, then we go around talking about why our life is so bad, then we kinesthetically connect (feel bad), and then our actions follow suit. Like I said earlier—same process, just the opposite outcome. Whatever we *see, say, feel,* and *do* . . . we *get!*

See It! Say It! Feel It! Do It!

This simple four-step strategy became the very process I needed to support me in changing any behavior that no longer served me. The following examples show how powerful this strategy can be, while giving you a simple explanation of the very complex happenings of our *bodymind* (thank you, Dr. Pert).

I want to start with an example that at first may seem irrelevant to you, especially if it doesn't apply to you specifically. But that is exactly why I have chosen it. It is not about the specific example; it's about getting the strategy, regardless of what we want to work on. I'm going to start with a habit that affects millions of people. Do you know anyone who bites his or her fingernails? (Or are you, perhaps, one of those people?) It may not seem like the most pleasant topic; however, it is an insidious habit because most people who bite their nails do so unconsciously. I was not an exception — I was a very competitive little miss in the days when I was a nail-biter. Nail-biting was something I had done for as long as I could remember, and I was the queen of nail-biters! And I came from a family of nail-biters.

When we're born, approximately 15 percent of our neural "wiring" is already in place. We have preestablished neural pathways, a genetic predisposition from our parents and their parents and so forth. I was born with a predisposition to nail-biting. I had a skinny little neural pathway that said, "I am a nail-biter. I am a nail-biter." This neural pathway was reinforced every time I bit my nails or saw another person doing the same thing. *Neurons that fire together, wire together.** When I saw my family biting their nails, my young mind thought, "Mmm—a food supply right at the end of my fingertips!"

By the time I was in my mid-thirties, with that constant firing of neurons, I had built a very thick, strong neural pathway that supported my nail-biting without my even having to be consciously aware of the process. (This is true for many of the habits we carry into our adult life, whether it's eating foods that don't support our health, judgments about others' beliefs, angry outbursts, or any of the other bad habits that stop us from enjoying our life to the fullest.)

One morning I came into our family room, and there sat Harison, having a good chew on his nails. He was about three and a half at the time. I said, "Stop biting your nails," to which he replied with complete innocence, "Why? You do!" As I am not one of those people who follow the "Do as I say, not as I do" school of parenting, I said, "Thanks for the feedback!" and set about working out how I would stop this habit that had been in my family for generations. I also knew that I had to stop biting my nails while Harison was still in the birth-to-seven age group. Ages seven and under are the most crucial years for the development of our

---

* In 1949 Donald Hebb, a Canadian neuropsychologist, coined the expression: "Neurons that fire together, wire together." This has since become known as Hebb's law. This simply means that each time we repeat a certain behavior or thought, we strengthen the connection between that set of brain cells or neurons. Many neuroscience experts use this wording: when the brain changes, the mind changes; when the mind changes, the brain changes. How exciting it is that we can use our conscious mind to make lasting changes to our brain to bring about greater well-being and peace into our life!

children's belief systems. Children are easily influenced at this age, and I knew that whatever I *did* would impact him heavily. To beat the habit, I had to work through Flipman's Strategy.

I had to ask myself: What were the pictures, words, feelings, and actions I needed to take in order to support me in creating the outcome I wanted—which was long, healthy, unbitten nails?

One of the greatest strengths of being human is that we can have experiences in our head before we actually have them in real life. We're able to simulate an experience that we want in our future, all because of our brain's wonderful frontal lobe (more specifically the prefrontal cortex). Development of the frontal lobe is the most recent stage in the ongoing development of our brain. The frontal lobe allows us to be creative, decisive, focused, contemplative, and adaptable. It gives us a long attention span; a strengthened sense of self; disciplined behavior; individuality; proactiveness; an ability to make dreams, goals, and intents more real than what's happening externally and to learn from mistakes—the list goes on. My kids laugh when I say, "I'm in love with my frontal lobe!" But I want them to realize just how important our brain—and in particular, our frontal lobe—is to our overall quality of life. I'm always telling my kids about the importance of wearing a helmet during sporting activities and the damage that could occur if they were not to wear one. Our frontal lobe gives us the ability to imagine our future, so if we want to have a more fulfilling, positive life, we need to take ownership of the pictures, dialogues, feelings, and actions we create on a day-to-day basis.

Let's get back to overcoming that nail-biting habit and work through each of the four stages of Flipman's Strategy.

The first thing we need to do is create the four opposite, positive corollaries of the See, Say, Feel, and Do of the (negative) state of nail-biting. We need to focus on the result that we want and then create the visual, auditory, kinesthetic, and take-action stimuli that will give us that result *as if we had already achieved it*. Let's go through it step by step.

Flipman's Strategy

Fake it till you make it!

Fake the opposite thought, feeling, and behavior
to the negative thought, feeling, and behavior
you are experiencing.

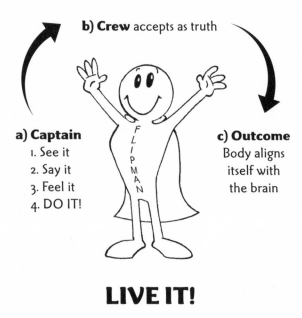

b) Crew accepts as truth

a) Captain
1. See it
2. Say it
3. Feel it
4. DO IT!

c) Outcome
Body aligns
itself with
the brain

LIVE IT!

Flipman's Strategy

1. **See It!**   Using positive visualization, make a *picture* in your mind of your hands with long, healthy nails—the more visual, the better. When you can make the picture as clear and as specific as possible, it's much easier for your mind to duplicate it. Having an actual picture of what you want to create can also help keep the visual really strong.

2. **Say It!**   Next, using a positive auditory stimulus, *tell* yourself, "I have long, healthy nails." It can be easy to think we have this part right, but I often hear people use a negative auditory stimulus such as "Stop biting your nails." Winning and not losing are two very different states, even though they may sound similar. One forces the mind to focus on the behavior of winning, and the other focuses on the behavior of losing. No one depicted this better than one of the greatest Flipman role models we have ever seen, Mother Teresa. She said, "I was once asked why I don't participate in anti-war demonstrations. I said that I will never do that, but as soon as you have a pro-peace rally, I'll be there." Can you see the difference? One directs energy toward war; the other directs energy toward peace. That's the power of effective dialogue! This is such an important part of the strategy that I have expanded on it further in the following pages.

3. **Feel It!**   Now, imagine how you will *feel* in the future when you look at your long, healthy nails (kinesthetic stimulus). This is the one step that most people leave out; either

they intellectualize it (just think it) or they avoid it because they feel silly acting out a feeling that isn't real. Yet this is probably the most important part of Flipman's Strategy. When we pretend to have the feeling of achievement and do it with the best acting skills we can muster, we help the brain send a message to the body that connects at the cellular level. Your brain thinks you already have achieved what you feel, so it supports the neural pathway production.

4. Do It!   Finally, you must keep fingernails out of your mouth. Take actions that support the outcome of long, healthy nails—we need to live as a person who has long, healthy nails and not wait until we actually have them.

So off I went with my new Flipman Strategy: "I have long, healthy nails . . . I have long, healthy nails." I kept pictures of long, beautiful nails around me, and I imagined feeling incredibly proud as I saw long, healthy nails on my fingers. I pretended (faked) that feeling. I even jumped in the air with joy at the thought of having long, healthy nails. Then, and most important, I would act like a person who doesn't bite her nails. I had my nails (such as they were at that point) manicured. I painted them with nail strengtheners, and each day I would feel myself achieving long, healthy nails. Now, as I look at my hands, I have long, healthy nails. I've had them for the past thirteen or so years! By continually repeating the process, over and over, I kept firing the neurons. (Remember, neurons that fire together, wire together.) And I finally created a new neural pathway of "I have long, healthy nails," which replaced the old dominant pathway of "I am a nail-biter."

For the really old habits, it can take approximately a thousand repetitions to create a really strong new neural pathway. So if we do a new behavior once a day, every day, it will take three years. That challenging time commitment alone can have us retreating to our old ways faster than a lizard drinking at a waterhole! But if we are serious about making long-lasting changes in our life, we'll do whatever it takes to make that happen.

I should point out that this is a very simple explanation of the far more complex phenomenon called "neuroplasticity." The most current research in neuroplasticity shows that we don't actually lose the old pathway; it simply lies dormant until we become stressed, and the temptation (Pitman) to revert to our old habits rears its ugly head. This is why so many of us slip back into our old habits when we experience stressful times in our lives. However, if we're aware of this temptation and have Flipman's Strategy in place, we'll be more likely to stick to our new healthy habits.

It's What You Say

As Flipman's Strategy shows, our perception and how we use language is so important. Step 2 in Flipman's Strategy (Say It!) is about how we dialogue what we want. Effective dialogue can mean the difference between achieving our goals and not, so we're going to look at this step of the strategy in more detail.

Using the nail-biting example, a lot of us would start by saying something like "Stop biting your nails." But wait.

Look at this statement carefully. The unconscious mind makes a picture—that is, it focuses on the behavior, not the command. So when we say, "Stop [command—Captain] biting your nails [behavior]," our mind has to first make a picture of biting the nails in order to stop. Once that picture is created, the unconscious mind immediately thinks that's what you want [Crew] because that's the picture you made, so the neurons fire once again as a nail-biter, even though we *think* we're doing the opposite.

Another common example of unconscious ineffective dialogue is when we pour a child a glass of milk. Some of us say, almost habitually, "Now, don't spill the milk." Just as soon as the words are out of our mouth, the milk is all over the floor. "I specifically told you not to spill the milk!" The child thinks, "Wow, Dad's a clairvoyant." So what happened? When you said, "Don't spill the milk," the child had to make a *picture* of spilling the milk in his or her mind in order not to (by which time it's too late). The unconscious mind received the data, the body aligned, and *whammo*, milk was everywhere. It's the same when people use negative dialogue, such as, "I'll never be able to stop smoking." Listen to that! The unconscious mind just says, "OK. You know far better than I do."

It's the same with expressions like, "I always . . ." or "I can't . . ." or "I find it so hard to . . ." In our house, we're not allowed to say, "I can't." We must instead say, "I am" or "I have." ("I have long, healthy nails! I have long, healthy nails! I have long, healthy nails!") As we have discussed, to take ownership of creating a new future for ourselves, we need to focus on the end result that we want and then language it as if we already have it:

I Am . . . I Have . . .

The younger we are when we learn this, the better! When Harison was about four, he walked into the kitchen, all slumped over (in the Pit), saying, "I can't find Thomas the Tank Engine, Mama! I can't find Thomas!"

I knelt down to his eye level and said, "Harison, remember, we don't say 'I can't' in this house. We say—"

Before I could finish, his eyes lit up, and he jumped in with, "I *am* finding Thomas, I *am* finding Thomas." After I left the room, I could hear him searching in his toy box, enthusiastically chanting, "I *am* finding Thomas, I *am* finding Thomas." Next, there was a squeal of delight, followed by "I found him!"

Then I asked, "How was that?"

"Worth it!" he shouted back. That was our little dialogue to encourage our boys to persist at things instead of choosing to quit.

Jackson is a little different from Harison, though. When he was about three, he was having trouble doing up the buttons on his shirt.

"I can't do up my buttons, Mama! I can't do up my buttons."

I responded with the usual, "We don't say 'I can't,' we say . . . ?"

He angrily shouted, "No more 'I am'—I said I *can't*!"

I just burst into laughter—Flipman's Strategy can have its funny moments. I realized we'd have to give this little guy a bit more time.

Another story that comes to mind is when Jackson was looking high and low in his bedroom for "Huggy" (the little security blanket he'd had since birth). He shouted out to me, "Mama, I can't find my huggy! I keep saying, 'I *am* finding my huggy, I *am* finding my huggy'—but I just can't find it!"

I replied with a chuckle, "That's because it's in the car!"

Pay the Price and Pay Attention

You may be saying, "Well, that's all fine and good with something as simple as nail-biting" (try telling that to a nail-biter!) "or looking for a toy train, but I can't see how it would help me with really strong habits." Let's take smoking as another example.

I, too, had my doubts that Flipman's Strategy would work for smoking. I was a very heavy smoker for many years. I started smoking when I was nineteen, and I remember that at the time my Pitman told me it would be *easy* for me to stop any time, if I wanted. How foolish I was to listen! I would smoke as fast as I spoke, and sometimes I'd have one resting on the ashtray, unnoticed, while lighting another. It didn't matter how hard I tried to quit, it seemed as if these little white sticks had complete control over me, even though my father died from lung cancer at forty-eight years of age. When you're nineteen, forty-eight can seem an eternity away, but as you get older, you realize just how young that really is. And as for the belief systems that form between birth and age seven—well, five out of my father's six children became heavy smokers! I thought I would never be able to quit smoking, and I used to fear that I would end up with lung cancer like my father.

But life has a wonderful way of helping us out if we *pay*

the price and pay attention. We need to keep listening for the messages that life brings us—and to do whatever we can to remove the distracting noise of blame, victimhood, and Pitman. (I was soon to receive some unmistakable messages, as you will see.)

Some of these messages come as a little metaphoric tap on the shoulder to capture our attention. Life doesn't want us to experience great pain and suffering in our learning, but if we're not paying attention, then it will get our attention any way it can! If we don't respond to the tap, we'll get a slap. If we don't pay attention to the slap, then we'll get a punch. If we don't pay attention to the punch, then it will be a sledgehammer, and if we're still not listening, a Mack truck will come along and smack us fair and square in the face and say, *"Now will you listen?"*

Think about it. When do most of us decide to get our health on track? When we get a health scare. When do most people read a book about relationships? That's right—when the partner has packed her bags and is headed out the door. We turn the pages of the book and acknowledge, "Hmm, so that's what went wrong. Page 32 had the answer. Bummer—two weeks too late!"

For most people, the Mack truck experience is a crisis situation. In my case, within the space of one week I met four people who had throat cancer. Then, as if the message wasn't clear enough for me, a woman came up to me during a coffee break during one of our training programs. She was in tears as she grabbed my arm and, with fear written across her face, said, "Terry, put that stupid cigarette out! My husband has just been diagnosed with cancer of the esophagus." Well, you could have knocked

me over with a feather. In that moment, I knew I would
never again have another cigarette. I don't know why it
was that moment, but it was as if I just woke up. That's
the best way I can describe my experience. It was another
satori, another instant awakening. It was as if all the lights
had been turned on for me in that one moment. Wow! But
then I thought, "Now that I've made this powerful decision, how on earth am I going to quit these horrid things?"

Then I remembered Flipman's Strategy. Yay! "Flipman
will help me through!" Still, I feared that Flipman might
not be enough. What if he didn't work for me, after all the
time I'd spent preaching about him to others? I didn't feel
that confident. But the wonderful thing about Flipman is
that you don't have to feel it to succeed. You just have to
do it — you have to do all four parts of Flipman's Strategy.

So again, let's work through this one together. I want
you to learn the strategy so that you not only understand
it but also remember it. That's why I am giving you a few
examples — so that you have practice using it to create powerful new habits.

What could be the positive See (visual), Say (auditory),
Feel (kinesthetic), and Do (take action) aspects that would
combat my negative feelings, thoughts, and behaviors of
wanting a cigarette? (Be careful not to slip back into old
dialogue habits — like "Don't smoke! Stop smoking!"
Remember, the mind makes a picture of the behavior.)

Important Tip: Even though we're not actually there
yet, think about where we want to end up. Some people
might say, "A nonsmoker with healthy, pink lungs," but
this is an outcome. Ask yourself, which pictures, words,

feelings, and actions do I need, to support me in creating the opposite of being a smoker? If you're struggling for an answer, I'm thrilled. It means that you're beginning to realize that although the formula may sound easy, it's not quite so easy to put into practice. We've spent years and years using inappropriate dialogue—and one of the dangers here is to assume that we already know this. There's a wonderful saying: "Some people are so far behind, they think they're out in front." We need to be cautious in our rush to "get" this. It is far better to go slow and allow ourselves the patience to really integrate this information.

We don't spend enough time focusing on our own dialogue. We pay insufficient attention to the unhealthy thinking, speaking, and doing habits that we pick up along the way.

Remember, neurons that fire together . . . it's the same for both *unhealthy* and *healthy* neural pathways.

So let me ask you, "What do nonsmokers hate?"

"Smokers!" people normally respond. We don't hate the smoker; we hate the smell of the smoke. (Love the criminal, hate the crime!)

See It!

So using visualization, let's *picture* ourselves being physically sick when we smell cigarette smoke (the more visual, the better).

Say It!

Next, using an auditory stimulus, we *tell* ourselves, "The smell of cigarette smoke makes me sick."

Feel It!

Now we imagine a *feeling* of nausea when we smell it (kinesthetic stimulus).

Do It!

And then we *walk away* from the temptation.

I used this exact method. I would recite to myself over and over, "The smell of cigarette smoke makes me sick, the smell of cigarette smoke makes me sick, the smell of cigarette smoke makes me sick . . ." In addition, I imagined a nauseous feeling and pictured myself being physically sick. Well, do you think it made me sick for the first few weeks? Not on your life! For the first few weeks, I would walk past a smoker hoping they would breathe out when I breathed in — *mmmmm, beautiful!* But inside my head, I persisted with Flipman's Strategy: "The smell of cigarette smoke makes me sick, the smell of cigarette smoke makes me sick, the smell of cigarette smoke makes me sick . . ." because my unconscious mind didn't know any different.

About six weeks later, after landing from a midnight-to-dawn flight, I stepped out of Sydney Airport and walked past a group of smokers at the front entrance. Without thinking, I took in a breath and felt physically sick — at last! I even dry retched! Let me tell you, I did a happy dance all the way to the car. "The smell of cigarette smoke really makes me sick — yay!" It was music to my ears. And to this day, the smell of smoke continues to make me feel nauseous, and I love that!

A couple of years after I had stopped smoking, my partner and I were at a dinner party, and I had eaten way too much. One of the guests lit up a cigarette, and in an instant

Pitman was circling around me, whispering in his seductive voice, *"Gee, it would be nice to have a cigarette right now!"* Aaaagh, Pitman! He was trying to sneak back in! *"One won't hurt you. Just have one. You'll be OK."*

No, Pitman, you will not get back in! As an excuse to leave the scene of the crime—an oh-so-familiar situation that was resurrecting those old neural pathways like a horde of ravenous zombies—I picked up a couple of empty glasses from the table and removed myself from the temptation. Inside my head, my inner voice said loud and clear, *"The smell of cigarette smoke makes me sick,"* just making sure that not one little urge could leak its way back in.

We have to pay a price in life. I know I keep saying this, but it is so important. We have to *pay attention!* These stories are not about me, and they're not about smoking or nail-biting (those are just examples). They're about *you* and about anything in your life that's stopping you from moving forward. I'm not telling you to quit smoking, nor am I judging smokers. Do whatever you want to do, but when you're ready to make any changes to your life, Flipman will help. We won't help ourselves by making a choice to smoke and then feeling guilty—that's doubly toxic. The most important part in all of this is the decisions we make about the life we want to create.

"I Only Have a Glass a Night!"

Drinking alcohol is another example from my own life that gave me the opportunity to use Flipman's Strategy. There was a time when I would come home from work in the evening and have one glass, two glasses, sometimes more than that. People would ask me, "How much do you drink a night?" I would answer jokingly, "I only have a glass a night. It's not my fault it's shaped like a bottle! Why pour when you can straw!" But behind the joking, I knew deep down that drinking alcohol was not serving me well. It was really a bit like soda pop to me, and I would use the excuse that I was just a bit of a party girl!

Being pregnant gave me good practice at going without alcohol, and I cut down a lot after having my babies, so that I was drinking only a couple of glasses of wine mixed with club soda in the evening. But I still needed those couple of glasses just to take the edge off. Looking back, I have to say that I've consumed a lot of alcohol since I started drinking at eighteen (the legal drinking age in Australia). I was not alone with my nightly drinking ritual; I'm sure that many readers can relate from their own experience. I have known many people who consume alcohol every day and feel they have it completely under control. Yet when faced with the prospect of not drinking for a certain period, the cold reality of their possible dependency is revealed.

I am not passing judgment here; our daily drinking habits are certainly a personal choice. I simply want to be sure that we don't hide from our reality by being in denial or using the "Oh, that's not me!" excuse. It can be so easy to dismiss our habitual behaviors by justifying the truth away. I, for example, would tell myself all the time, "It's only a couple of glasses. Relax, it's not that bad!"

When my older brother died at the age of forty-three from alcohol-related liver failure, I became strongly motivated to do something about my personal habits. Just as smoking had had a hold on me, it seemed impossible to contemplate a life without alcohol; I really felt that I needed those couple of glasses each evening. Yet there was something deep inside telling me that alcohol was incompatible with my life goals and my personal values.

As luck would have it—and this was my sledgehammer—a few years after my brother's death, I went to see a doctor because I wasn't feeling too good. She ran a few tests and discovered that I had become infected with quite a serious parasite. "I can't have," I laughed. "That old boyfriend left years ago!" She laughed too, but then she said that she was very concerned about my condition and recommended that I undergo a heavy course of antibiotics. She then added that because of the high dosage, I was not to drink alcohol for four whole weeks!

Everything seemed to go into slow motion. "Hooooow loooooong did you say?" I asked, hoping that I'd misheard and that she had really said only four hours!

"Four weeks," she repeated firmly.

"What? Four whole weeks?" I found this very confronting. I kept weighing it. Drinking—parasite—drinking—parasite . . . Maybe if I drank enough alcohol, I would kill the parasite! Joking aside, I really was confronted by the two options that lay before me—my health or my alcohol habit—and to be honest, I found it a very difficult choice to make. Even though I knew deep down I would ultimately choose my health, I was angry that I had to give up something that I enjoyed and felt I needed—for four long weeks. I had never experienced adult life without alcohol.

It can sound so pathetic when we play it back to ourselves, but when anything has a hold of you, it can be very hard to let it go, even if it isn't good for you. This was an incredibly confronting situation for me. My liver was not as healthy as it should have been, and my brother's death was a pretty strong influence, so in the end, I chose my health. The hardest part for me was the first few days. I even held a ceremonial dinner the night before I quit, and I marked my calendar for four weeks later, to the day. Day one was tough, day two was a bit worse, day three got a little easier, and as each day went on, I felt myself gaining new strength. Every day, I focused on Flipman's Strategy:

See It!
I could see myself at the end of the four weeks, alcohol-free.

Say It!
The dialogue was easy: "I am on medication and not allowed alcohol."

Feel It!
Each day, I would imagine I was at the end of the four weeks and feeling fabulous!

Do It!
Each day, I chose to drink club soda and lemon in a wine glass, no ice!

The four weeks were over before I knew it, and I felt healthier, clearer, and so much more empowered. I felt like I had come alive. Not only had my skin tone dramatically improved, but my mental clarity had never been sharper! And the fact that I had followed through for the entire four weeks gave me a powerful sense of pride in myself. I had kept my word. Encouraged by this renewed strength, I decided to persist with my course of abstinence. I didn't know how I would fare, so I didn't put any pressure on myself. I decided that if I really felt like having a drink, I would simply have one. Initially my dialogue had been "I'm not drinking because I'm taking medication," so I changed it to "I'm alcohol-free at the moment."

Little did I realize that my last alcoholic drink would turn out to be the one I had on August 9, 2003. If you had told me that night at dinner that I would never drink again, I would have laughed. I am so grateful for that parasite! Now, when I'm asked, I simply reply that I only drink non-alcoholic drinks. My wiring has completely changed, to the extent that I no longer can stand the smell of certain alcoholic beverages. At a conference dinner one evening, one of the delegates commented on how strong I must be to refrain from drinking at "events like this." That's when it clicked about my wiring, and as I explained to him, it isn't even a conscious choice for me anymore. And then I had another amazing realization.

I've heard that some support groups use phrases like "I *am* an alcoholic. I *am* an incest survivor. I *am* an over-eater," and so on. In my opinion, this dialogue just keeps reinforcing the negative patterns of the past. It reinforces the wiring. Why would anyone keep reminding himself or herself of the very thing they want to be rid of? I'm not an expert on the psychology or science of addictions, but I do know that anything that can support a positive outcome must be of benefit. Whichever word we place after "I *am* . . . ," we reinforce. We fire those neurons, making the pathway stronger and stronger. Such phrases do not serve us in rewiring our pathways in a powerful way. They keep people constantly focusing on what they *don't* want, not what they *do* want.

Please understand that I do *not* mean to criticize any support group and the tireless work they do for their members. I just think that sometimes we can get stuck in the way we have always done it—results are results, and my goal, especially when it comes to our health and well-being, is to keep looking for ways that give us a better outcome. I could have easily left this part out of the book, for fear of offending people. But one has to ask, why do we get offended? If we get heat for speaking up, let's look at it and not be blinded by our beliefs, which may have become outdated without our even noticing. Remember, we once thought the world was flat. It would be foolish to think we know it *all* now. I am just asking that we contemplate our current beliefs to check whether they still serve us in achieving our goals.

At this point in my life, I see myself never drinking alcohol again. Do I miss it? Not at all. I was actually amazed at how easy it was to completely stop—although I do admit that in the early days, there was the occasional evening when I felt that a long glass of icy cold champagne would have slid down beautifully. I'm not suggesting that we should have an alcohol-free world. I'm only speaking for myself here: I'm simply not good with alcohol. Alcohol doesn't work for me, and it doesn't fit with the way I live my life anymore. Again, I am not saying to you, "Don't drink." Your constitution may be completely different from mine. Being a nondrinker is a great choice for me because I didn't like who I became when I drank. You may be completely different. Just be totally honest with yourself. Deep down, there's a part of you that knows the truth, and that part knows whether you're using a substance to push away whatever you're running from.

When we use anything to numb ourselves to the reality of our issues (food, drugs, alcohol, anger, work, chocolate, the Pit, and so on), we're not getting rid of problems — we're just pushing them down. The moment we stop the habit, up they come! My greatest realization was that drinking numbed me. I didn't have to face my "stuff." My problems and issues became less important after my nightly couple of glasses. Alcohol became like a mild sedative, and I lived a lot of my nights in a gentle haze, which of course I didn't realize until I stopped drinking. When I stopped drinking, everything I had been pushing down came up, and I was now faced with the ordeal of dealing with my stuff.

But now that I had a clear head, the most amazing thing was how much easier it was for me to deal with the very issues I had been drinking to avoid. I think that the saddest part of our current society is that we don't let our stuff come up, whatever these issues may be. We forget that we have put a lot of repetitions into creating the unwanted behaviors, so we also need to put a lot of repetitions into creating the new, wanted behaviors.

I heard someone describe creating new neural pathways as being similar to creating a new waterfall. How do some waterfalls begin? With one drop of water, and then another and another and another — until one day there's such a massive force of billions and billions of drops of water that a waterfall is formed. But we're not used to doing it the tough way. We've been spoiled by the quick and easy solutions prevalent in our current society.

Dare to Delve

Many years ago, I wasn't sleeping very well because my eating habits weren't that great, I had been flying a lot for work, and my then-husband was a big snorer. After quite a few weeks of sleep deprivation, I felt exhausted. I also had an extremely painful right shoulder and elbow, which worked in tandem with the snoring to ensure that some nights I had no sleep at all. All of this, *plus* I was working full-time and had two little boys (I sound like a bit of a Pitman, don't I?).

I dragged myself off to the doctor in search of a remedy for my lack of sleep. By this stage I was very teary and a bit spacey—I felt like I had been hit by a truck! After a few minutes of consultation, the doctor prescribed antidepressants.

"But why?" I questioned in shock. I had no reason to be depressed. I had a loving marriage, two great toddlers, and a fulfilling business, and I was happy with my life. "I certainly don't feel depressed!" I said.

The doctor replied, "I think you're not sleeping because you're depressed."

I was absolutely dumbfounded by this diagnosis. So I clarified what he'd said: "You're saying I'm not sleeping because I'm sad, is that right?"

"Yes," he replied confidently.

"Might it be the other way around—that I'm sad because I'm not sleeping?" I said through gritted teeth. He became quite irritated that I had questioned his diagnosis. And I was annoyed that he prescribed antidepressants so casually, without discussing my diet, exercise, or lifestyle or running any tests. He knew nothing about my personal life, my eating habits, or anything else about me, period! (Back then, my attitude about exercise was simply, "Why walk when there's a good car parked outside!") And there he sat, happy to tell me that I needed antidepressants, while offering no other tests, no other form of therapy, or any other relief for my sleeplessness.

I'm not saying there isn't a place for antidepressants. If they're going to prevent someone from taking their own life or if they're going to give someone a jolt from a habitual Pitman state, then I say go for it—but they shouldn't be prescribed that casually.

I walked out of my doctor's office completely disillusioned. When I had a chance to clear my head, I thought, "How dare anyone so easily play with my body and my life like that!" It wasn't until many years later that I discovered I had contracted an autoimmune condition—and that my profound exhaustion, depression, sense of loathing, anxiety, and painful right shoulder were just a few of the symptoms! I am so grateful that I trusted my inner guide. I knew I wasn't depressed, but I also knew something was wrong.

Love yourself enough to keep asking. Trust yourself enough to know that you know you better than anybody. Dare to delve into your own life. We will talk about this more in Chapter 14, but for now I urge you to dare to be the explorer and search for the deeper meaning rather than just doing a quick cover of those "taps on the shoulder" concerning drugs, food, work, alcohol, or things. As Scott Peck's wonderful book title says so eloquently, take *The Road Less Traveled*. Also, teach your children to take the tougher, more challenging road. Show them that walking through our pain teaches us to be resilient. We become much braver and more courageous by facing our pain instead of numbing it, and we also create far more opportunities for ourselves.

Flipman Is a Choice!

Changing our old habits into new, more positive and empowering ones can take a lot of commitment and dedication. Life is challenging! Being a parent is challenging, being married is challenging, being single is challenging, being twelve is challenging, being seventy is challenging, running a company is challenging, running two miles is challenging—life is challenging! There are no free lunches in this world. When we start to accept that life is challenging, everything begins to get easier. We stop looking for an easy way out and accept that there's work to be done, and Flipman can help us accomplish these goals.

Over the years, I've heard countless stories from people about how Flipman has influenced their life: from losing weight to quitting smoking; from saving a person's life to becoming the number-one salesperson in the firm; from healing themselves from an illness to falling back in love with their partner. People have shown me that Flipman 'n the choices we make in each moment.

At a client function, I ran into someone whom I had trained a few years back. She was so excited; she wanted to share a story about her final exam to qualify as a firefighter.

A building was on fire, and my partner was inside. My task was to find my partner and get him out of the burning building. This was my last task before becoming a fully qualified firefighter, and I had trained so hard for this moment. I had only a certain amount of time, and for some reason, the heat, the pressure, the race against time started to have a negative effect on me. I started to panic. My breath became short, I couldn't find my partner, and I felt like I was burning up. It was awful, and I was about to give in and give up when I remembered!

You should have seen the look on her face as she shared her story. I had goose bumps on my arms and tears in my eyes.

She continued,

I knew that if I just focused on Flipman, I would be OK. I was still terrified, but I concentrated on slowing my breathing. In, out, in, out. My heart was pounding so hard I thought it was going to burst through my chest, but I kept breathing in, out, in, out. I then clearly visualized myself finding my partner. I started moving forward into the fire, saying out loud, "*I am finding my partner! I am finding my partner!*" Within what felt like a few seconds, my partner appeared before my eyes. We got out of that fire, and I passed my test! I love Flipman!

As she finished, we fell into a beautiful hug.

That story still inspires me today. I love Flipman too, and the number of situations where he turns up never ceases to amaze me. Flipman isn't there for us only in life-threatening situations; he can also be with us in ordinary, stressful day-to-day situations.

It's wonderfully empowering when we not only learn these strategies but also implement them to help to create the life that we want. This can kindle a passionate enthusiasm for sharing this knowledge with those we share our life with. In the next chapter, we'll take a look at how to do this by *being* a Flipman example rather than by calling out others' Pitman behaviors.

Chapter 13

The Best Way to Teach Is to *Be!*

Every day we make the choice about where and how we will spend our day. *We* decide whether we want to be a Flipman, and when we do, we become far more aware of the Pit behaviors of the people around us. It can be hard to resist the temptation to judge them. I hope no one reads this book, then walks up to the first energy sucker he or she meets and says, "Hey, Pitman, I've got some 'feedback' for you!" I'm sure we all realize by now that this is about working on our own stuff and not about criticizing someone else. When we're busy criticizing someone else's backyard, we're usually allowing weeds to grow in our own.

One of the most annoying things we can do to someone is to become the Pit Police! I don't know too many people who respond well to someone being overly critical of their behavior. It all comes back to our intention. If we want to pass harsh judgment on a person's behavior by labeling them a Pit Person in public, then we're probably the one who should be wearing the Pitman name badge! If our intention is to help someone see his or her limiting behaviors with respect and kindness, then we will usually find the most appropriate approach to use.

We may have the best of intentions to "save" the Pit People in our lives, but we must remember that no one can help those who are in their Pit; they have to help themselves. When we give up the illusion that we're the reason someone climbs out of his or her Pit, we move from the dangerous rescuer role into the more successful empowerment role. The same applies to us: no one is going to save us. It is our choice, our dialogue, and our behavior that place our foot on that first rung of the ladder. For now, the best thing we can do is to "get this" for ourselves. Of course we can offer advice and guidance to another, but the choice to change is not ours, it's theirs. The most powerful way to influence another person is through our actions. People follow what we do, not what we say, and being is the outcome of doing — *so the best way to teach is to be.*

Be *loving and respectful* as a parent, if you want more loving and respectful kids.

Be *present and attentive* as a partner, if you want the same from your partner.

Be *hardworking, honest, and participative* as an employer, if this is the behavior you want from your employees.

Be *peaceful, kind, generous, and forgiving,* if you want a more peaceful, kind, generous, and forgiving world.

We all need to find that Flipman warrior within us. If you think about it, what is a warrior? A warrior is respectful.

A warrior has honor, and a warrior slays a dragon only if there is a dragon to be slain. If there's no dragon in front of the warrior, he or she puts down the sword. Warriors do not go out and fight just for the sake of fighting, but if they need to stand there and deal with the challenging moments in their life, they do it.

Some of us can become negative when we're learning new things or letting go of outdated behaviors, reactions, or responses. This process is a bit like having to walk through a wild, uninhabited jungle that's in front of us. Imagine massive trees and wild weeds and a whole impenetrable-seeming jungle. All we have as a warrior is our sword (our Flipman courage, honesty, and faith), and as we continue, the only way out of this jungle is through. We can't go around it. We can't go over it. We can't go under it. We've got to go through the jungle. So we slash through the jungle. We cut the weeds in front of us. We bring down the limiting beliefs that are blocking our path, and when we look back, it's basically a cleared area. Once we're through the jungle, we actually come to a lovely, open grassy patch where we can rest. Isn't that how life happens?

When I'm right in the middle of my "jungle," I sometimes think, "How much longer is this jungle going to go on for? How much more do I have to learn? Why is it so frustrating? Why can't things be easier? How am I going to be able to keep coping with this pain? When will this pass?"

I soon realize that if I just get on with the task at hand, go into the pain, and deal with whatever issues come up, I will always come out on the other side to the grassy patch. I always come out to somewhere where I can rest. The grass is just a past jungle that we've already mastered. So it will always be there for us. We'll always come to a place where we can rest.

Pain Is a Pathway

One of the most powerful epiphanies I have ever had was when I realized that pain offers the doorway to our breakthroughs. Would it not make sense then to learn how to *do* pain well? Think about every area of life—if we want to be fit and healthy, we need to experience the pain that can come with working our bodies hard and saying no to the foods that are unhealthy, while we grow new neural pathways that love the taste of delicious, healthy foods.

What about financial freedom? By working through the pain of delayed gratification, we learn to wait until we can pay for something instead of getting ourselves deeper and deeper into debt, which invariably causes much worse pain. What about our relationships? If we want to take our relationship to the next level, there is bound to be pain involved—especially with those tough, honest conversations. And what if we run a business? There is always pain if we are implementing a new strategy or policy, or even if we're just asking our people to produce more.

Change of any kind can cause pain, and because of that, most of us have learned to fear change. Pain is part of the process, and by trying to avoid it, we just prolong the inevitable. The faster we learn how to experience the pain, push through it, and learn what action we have to take, the sooner we will come out the other side with much more wisdom, resilience, and gratitude for what we have achieved and received.

Fear Is Just a Feeling

Our physical body uses pain as a warning sign to pay attention. Does it not make sense, then, that our emotional body is sending us an important message as well? So many of us let our fear of pain paralyze us from moving forward, yet that fear really is just a feeling to be managed.

Fear is one of those words that most of us use as a reason for not achieving our goals, for not going through the jungle. I mentioned this in the beginning of the book as the excuse I used for not doing the recordings for Lynn, the client who wanted them as an aid in her grieving process. Guess how I perceive fear now? As a massive beating of my heart, a pounding in my chest. A *feeling!* That's what happens in my body when I'm fearful. So I've decided that whenever I'm fearful, my greatest job in that moment is to just manage my heartbeat. And the best way I know to do that is through breathing—deep, long, slow breaths. There have been times in my life when my anxiety and fear were so great that even breathing hurt. But I kept doing it because I knew that my greatest task in that moment was to manage my heartbeat. And sure enough, calmness returned, and I was OK—just as you will be.

This is the journey of a person living a Flipman life. Pitman urges us to just give up, doesn't he? He seduces us into thinking we can have an easier life: "Just accept things the way they are. That's the way it is. Don't dredge up the past. It's not your fault. You should get revenge for what was done to you. Someone has to pay for this! Don't they know what you've been through?"

Maybe the "jungle" for you is a tough conversation that

needs to be had. Maybe it's something you need to face within yourself. It may be a situation in which you need to state your truth, or it could be some part of your past that you need to accept and forgive. The greatest thing about all of us is that our soul needs to evolve, and surrendering to our personal evolution is like giving it oxygen. Whatever we need to deal with is not going to go away. It will keep coming back to hit us harder and harder, until we face it. And what a great role model you'll be for all those who follow you — the seen and the unseen.

It's worth saying again: The best way to teach is to *be*!

Chapter 14

Transition Time

Change is not achieved without inconvenience,
even from worse to better.

— RICHARD HOOKER, SIXTEENTH-CENTURY
THEOLOGIAN

I love that saying because I think many of us expect change to be a lot easier than it is, especially when we're right in the middle of it. We make these grand changes to our life, thinking they're for the better, and quite often our life gets worse or more uncomfortable, even painful, before it starts to improve. Many people don't achieve long-term success but keep returning to the Pit in large part because they don't ride out the transition time — the period from the old behaviors or patterns to the new ones that are forming.

Remember, there is no failure, only feedback, and feedback is a necessary part of the success journey — the journey of uncovering the wonderful mystery called *you*! Few of us achieve what we want after the first attempt, but we can fall into the trap of allowing ourselves to get discouraged. We expect the transition to be easy, and it's not. It can be incredibly challenging at times, not to mention painful, and Pitman is there the whole way, coaxing, seducing, urging us back to our old ways, saying things like:

"Have a puff on that cigarette — one puff won't hurt!"

"Lose your temper with your kids/staff/lover. They don't realize how hard you work!"

"Have an extra piece of chocolate cake; you deserve it!"

"Sleep in; you can go to the gym tomorrow!"

"Feel sorry for yourself. No one cares anyway!"

"Have that extra drink; you need something to calm yourself!"

"Withdraw from those who love you; they don't understand!"

"Forget about finishing this job; you can do it later."

We have to be aware of Pitman's presence and to allow Flipman to take over. We must constantly be aware of the urge to surrender to the "easy" way. We already know that the way to get out of a Pitman frame of mind is to *do* a positive behavior, thought, and feeling that is opposite to what we're negatively feeling or thinking. If I'm feeling irritable, I force myself to smile and be lovely to people. If I feel like I want to quit some work I'm doing because it's "too hard," I force myself to keep going. If I feel like stopping my run or weight session, I force myself to keep doing one lift after the next. If I feel like quitting anything, I force myself to stick with it. Do I always succeed? No. There is always a transition period. I do know, though, that I'm 100 percent responsible for the choices I make in each moment, and the subsequent outcomes.

One of the easiest ways we can try to skip the discomfort and pain of the transition phase of a relationship breakup, without even realizing it, is to try to create another relationship. After the initial adjustment of separating from my husband and adapting to my new single life, I found myself unconsciously looking for a potential partner. I would get on a plane and scan the cabin for any man I was attracted to, and then I would check his left hand. Wedding ring? Yes. Oh well. *Next!* I had spent the previous eighteen years with someone in my life. I didn't know how to be single anymore, so I kept searching everywhere I went.

With the wisdom of hindsight, I can see how in the first few months I was doing everything I could to avoid the painful transition time from being married to being single. Even though I had chosen to be single, I would hate nights on the sofa by myself. I was doing everything I could to avoid the inevitable. Then one night, when I was feeling particularly vulnerable, it hit me! I realized that I had kept myself so busy that I hadn't fully acknowledged to myself that I *was on my own*. That was the night I accepted that I was really single instead of waiting for someone to come in and fill that space! There wasn't anyone to chat with me, hear me out, sit with me, or hold and comfort me — not even anyone to fight with me!

I started to cry . . . and I cried and cried and cried. I was crying because I was scared about whether I could make it on my own. I was crying for what I had left behind, and I was crying because I felt so empty and uncertain. I was crying for my little boys and their heartache. It was one of the hardest periods of my life, but the only way out is through!

I had to walk through the pain; I had to go through my jungle. I had to stop waiting. I realized it was either now or too late!

I sobbed my eyes out . . . *and then I surrendered.*

I surrendered to the realization that I was on my own, and I accepted that this transition would probably be painful—gut-wrenchingly painful. I surrendered to the fact that I would feel lonely, yet this was a space I needed to get used to. The easiest thing for me would have been to go straight into another relationship, but that wouldn't have served me well for what I needed to learn. I needed to learn how to be on my own. I needed to learn how to look after myself. I needed to be able to stand on my own two feet and stop waiting for someone to come along and save me, as I had in all of my previous relationships. These thoughts terrified me, but I forged ahead all the same. It was like I was free-falling. I had nothing to cling to, and I was terrified yet exhilarated at the same time.

There were many moments when I just sat on the floor all alone and cried my eyes out. This was *not* a Pitman thing to do; it was an utterly Flipman thing to do—to express my emotions fully. I just allowed myself the right to feel what I needed to feel, without judgment. I wanted to understand me. I wanted to understand my needs and how I could be a better role model for my boys. I wanted to understand where my pain *really* came from and cease the blame game that had become too familiar in my dialogue.

I learned a lot, and I continue to do so. I also realized that I needed to give myself the space and time to adapt. Transition requires a great deal of focus, courage, and time. It's easy to be addicted to the familiar patterns of the past. It's a bit like having a "good enemy"; they're not necessarily good for us, but we know how to play the game, so we keep them. So many of us get stuck wanting that familiarity, even if it's to our own detriment.

Conquering Uncomfortable Emotions

When uncomfortable emotions arise in us, we tend to justify them away with Pitman comments, such as "I'm just tired," "I'm hormonal," "I have a headache," "I'm just not feeling myself," "I've just been so busy." When we do this, we ignore the profound truths that are waiting just under the surface. We need to pay attention to these patterns rather than flick them off as something that's out of our control. The moment we open the floodgates to our learning, and the moment we allow ourselves to take complete responsibility for our own evolution, it's nonstop. It's the most exhilarating experience in the world. There's a wonderful saying, "You can never be unenlightened!" We can never undo what we know, and if we're clever enough, we'll keep adding to this sense of knowing and create a powerful compounding effect.

Having said that, the transition time can feel very painful, scary, and even awkward at times, so you can easily pull away and give up just when you are about to have a breakthrough. A necessary part of having a successful transition from what you are to what you want to be is allowing yourself to become the explorer in your own life. Instead of shutting down when the going gets tough, push on with a determined attitude to uncover the mystery that is you. (Just manage that heartbeat.) Why wait to be great? It's either now or too late!

Another way of recognizing an opportunity for exploring is to notice what repulses us. Have you ever noticed that your reaction to something was not in line with the situation? When the punishment far outweighs the crime, there's usually an underlying unresolved issue. It's a signal for us to pay attention and do some serious exploring. Bring it in! The things we dislike in others are usually the things that we dislike in ourselves but are not willing to admit to. When we have a strong dislike for someone or get angry and act out with someone, and we don't know why, it's usually because something has come up for us but we're not willing to accept it yet. If we start to unravel our patterns, we also have to be willing to experience the consequences of doing so. The journey to self-awareness is the most challenging and arduous of our lives, and I think that's why most people continue to live in a state of numbness.

Peace and freedom happen when we let our Flipman shine through—especially the warrior part of Flipman. So often in my past, I did not allow my warrior to come through. The victim would come up. The poor wounded Pit Girl would come up. I would allow all this garbage from my past to stop me from being a true warrior. So one day I gave myself permission to be still and to have the time to contemplate. I now love time by myself (Me time). I cherish it. My alone time after the separation gave me the space to be my own explorer, to analyze my parenting, my leadership, and my friendships. Over time, I got to really know myself; I got to explore the reasons why I thought the way I did. I was able to evaluate the patterns that I had created in previous relationships, and I discovered what I did to attract these types of relationships into my life. During this period of transition and exploration, I also worked out how I wanted to be treated and what I would and would not settle for. I worked out what was important to me and what I expected from future relationships, and I defined the areas where I would no longer compromise.

Did this happen overnight? No way! But it did happen. I remember one night, about five months after the separation; the tears came up once again after saying goodbye to my boys for another week, as their father drove off with them. This happened every second week, and each time I would cry so hard it felt as though my heart was being wrenched out of my chest. But on that particular night, I made a decision: I had cried enough. There comes a time when we've grieved, cried, and worried enough, after which it's time to move on. The lights go on, and we wake up! Of course I was still going to miss my boys dreadfully whenever I wasn't with them, but I was no longer going to allow

When I go to the Pit,
I know it is my choice.

my feelings to paralyze me. We can get so stuck in our sadness that we can feel it's never going to pass.

Not long after the separation I was driving home one day feeling particularly sad. I was crying my eyes out once again, and believe me, I am not a quiet weeper! The pain in my heart was so enormous that I felt I could barely breathe. I was passing through a forest on my journey home, and I heard a voice in my head saying, "This too shall pass!" And I really believed it.

"This too shall pass! Happy does come back." Well, about two weeks later, I was driving past the exact same spot, but this time I felt amazing. I had the music pumping; I was on fire. Woo-hoo! And that same voice jumped into my head and said, "And this *too* shall pass!" I burst out laughing. How true is that? Every moment passes, and after night comes day, and when we're done with sadness, happy does comes back!

I know that I'll have many more times in my life when I'll be touched by events that will offer me an opportunity to transform who I am, and they may very well come disguised as painful experiences. We will all have such experiences. And I know that I won't always handle them with Flipman fortitude and grace. The great thing now, though, is that I decide when, where, with whom, and for how long I go to my Pit! I also give myself permission to feel all of my feelings, especially the healthy ones like sadness, grief, appropriate anger, and appropriate frustration. And when I go to the Pit, I am fully aware of it. I also know when I'm in there that it's no one else's fault.

Chapter 15

Our Book of Life

We started this book by talking about how living is a series of events, all joined together to form the great story of our life. From the time I was a young adult, I always likened the entirety of my life to a great big book, its pages filled with experiences, people, and adventures.

We each have our own Book of Life filled with our own stories and journeys. Some of our friends and family will be in our book for many chapters. Some may feature in only a few paragraphs; others will appear for only a few words. There's a wonderful saying—"People come into your life for a reason, a season, or a lifetime"—that beautifully describes our relationships through time. Every encounter, discussion, facial expression, and positive or nasty word to another human being goes into *their* Book of Life, and into ours as well.

I might feature in your Book of Life only for a couple of words, but let me tell you, if I am going to be in someone's book, I want to be 32-point **bold**, not 8-point faded *italic!* I want to make sure that I give everything I've got, as often as I can, to as many people as possible. We all have an effect on each other. Every interaction with another human being helps that person write his or her book, as it helps us write our own. We're in "metaphoric print" together forever.

The following story demonstrates the impact our influence has on another person's life. Versions have been widely circulated by e-mail and on the Web; according to snopes.com, it's "based on a longer first-person account given by Margaret Fishback Powers in her 1993 book *Footprints: The True Story Behind the Poem That Inspired Millions.*" Regardless of the origin or version, I'm sure all of us can relate to the power of its message. I'm reproducing it just as I received it.

> Some time ago, a mother punished her five-year-old daughter for wasting a roll of expensive gold wrapping paper. Money was tight, and she became even more upset when the child used the gold paper to decorate a box to put under the Christmas tree. Nevertheless, the little girl brought the gift box to her mother the next morning and said, "This is for you, Mama." The mother was embarrassed by her earlier overreaction, but her anger flared once more when she opened the box and found it was empty. She spoke to her daughter harshly. "Young lady, don't you know that when you give someone a present, there's supposed to be something inside the package?"
>
> The little girl's eyes filled with tears as she replied,

"Oh, Mama, it's not empty! I blew kisses into it until it was full."

The mother was crushed. She fell on her knees, put her arms around her little girl, and begged her forgiveness for her thoughtless anger.

A short time later, an accident took the life of this child. It is said that her mother kept that golden box by her bed all the years of her life. Whenever she was discouraged or faced difficult problems, she would open the box and take out an imaginary kiss and remember the love of the child who had put it there. In a very real sense, each of us has been given a Golden Box filled with unconditional love and kisses from our children, family, friends, and God. There is no more precious possession anyone could hold.

This story still moves me to tears. We all know times when we have said words that have crushed another person's spirit. We are all offered opportunities to touch another's heart and spirit, if we just take the time to notice.

Now that I live in the United States, I've noticed many people who are homeless and living on the street. It saddens me greatly. One day I passed a man on a street corner holding a sign that read, "SMILE, your life could be worse, it could be mine!"

It massaged my heart and brought a tear to my eye. He had such a happy face, and I couldn't get him or that sign out of my head. His simple sign made such an impression that I decided to post it on Flipman's Facebook page.

The next day when I drove past he was still there, so I

The Book of Life

stopped the car and gave him twenty dollars — not out of pity, but for using his material!

Since that experience, the boys and I have created a little dignity pack in which we put a copy of this book, a little Flipman, $10.00, and some dental hygiene products. Whenever we come across someone who is living homeless, we give him or her a pack and, whenever possible, have a conversation. As I drive off each time, I sincerely hope this book helps them to improve their situation. I also just love seeing my boys' faces, knowing they have helped one life to be a little easier, even if just for a moment.

Note: I am really clear about saying *people who are homeless*, not *homeless people*. I know this is a small detail, but I think it's important that we don't define anyone by their current situation. Life can change in a heartbeat.

We all can become so easily consumed in the drama of our own life that we stop seeing how we can help another. It doesn't have to cost anything, but I don't know any better way to lift my spirit and fill my heart than to help someone who might need a hand.

We all have the opportunity to touch another life, to throw a pebble of love, even if just for a moment. That moment may be just what that someone needed to turn the corner in life. Every day we have that metaphoric pen in our hand, ready to write.

So the next time you do or say anything, ask yourself, "How do I want to appear in this person's Book of Life?"

Chapter 16

Writing in Another's Book of Life

Some of the greatest chances for falling into the Pit arise through our interactions with other people. We may truly intend to write positive things in their Book of Life and then fall short of that intention. The good news is, there are things we can do to help put Flipman into action.

Being Right

As we now know, it is our interpretation of a situation that creates our response to it. In my younger, less informed years, I would often get myself all worked up by trying to convince someone of my opinion, especially if theirs didn't match mine! I would have passionate disagreements, thinking that if I could give a good enough argument, I could get them to see my point of view. But of course, I usually ended up jumping into my Pit and feeling frustrated and angry! I now look back and realize that my empathy skills needed a lot of work, and it wasn't so much the differing opinions that put me in the Pit as it was my insatiable desire to be right.

There is a wonderful saying, "What is more important, being right or having peace?" As I get older and continue to use my Flipman approach to life, I find that I'm becoming more mellow in my responses to certain situations. I now find myself letting things slide that I would have previously found incredibly irritating or upsetting. Wouldn't it have been great to discover that pearl of wisdom a little earlier in life so that I would not have wasted important energy on minor irritations and incidental issues?

I have often heard others say that as they mature they too have become mellower. I hope this characteristic isn't restricted to those who are maturing, but maybe life experience is the rite of passage.

I'm not saying we should be pushovers. I think respectful assertiveness and a healthy self-esteem are two of the most important traits anybody can possess. But when we're in our Pitman state, we can tend to feel that everyone else is against us, and to see every slight or conflict as a personal attack. "They did it to me!" When we're in that frame of mind, we can get so blinded by having to win the fight that we lose the war. How often does proving that we're right bring us peace? We lose sight of the big picture and get stuck in winning the argument. It might give us some sense of satisfaction, but at what cost?

It took me a long time to learn this powerful lesson. Again, this does not mean we become submissive. It's more about having the wisdom to let slide those things that don't really matter. Chapter 4 on empathy really explains this. When we can truly put ourselves in the place of another, we can easily see the situation through that person's eyes. We become less concerned with being right and more concerned with understanding. When we aim to understand, we usually create peace as a result. So when you're about to explode at someone important in your life, pause and consider which is more important to you: *being right* or *having peace?*

How to Have a Great Relationship

I have discovered the formula for creating a happy, fulfilling relationship, and it boils down to one simple sentence. Now, because I'm a divorced single mother, you may be thinking my advice on this is on a par with a vegetarian's advice on how to cook steak! But I've been around the block a few times, and after years of working with human beings and watching what works and what doesn't, I believe I *do* know the formula.

If we understand and accept the power of empathy in a relationship, this will be the next evolution for us because it will make sense. If it doesn't, then maybe we need to reevaluate how well we understand and accept the powerful role that empathy plays in our relationships.

Are you ready for this amazingly simple, one-sentence formula? Here it is:

Just find out what the other person wants to feel loved and give it to them!

Sounds simple, doesn't it? But is it? So often when we're in a relationship with someone, we assume we know what he or she wants. We often base our knowledge of their needs on our assumptions rather than on true understanding. If we've mastered the ability to see life through the eyes of our partner, our children, our friends, our customers, and so on, we're more likely to *want* to give them what they want rather than feeling we *have* to give.

A lengthy relationship is also no guarantee that we understand each other's needs. When was the last time we asked someone we love, "How do you know I love you?" What if someone asked the same of you? If we wanted to take our relationships to the next level, we could even continue with, "And how can I love you better?" We can usually articulate what makes us feel loved. If we ask the people we love, "How do you know I love you?" they'll probably tell us, so let's make sure we listen to their answers. They're telling us how they measure our love—whether we like it or not, whether it fits with our paradigm or not. And when they let us know how we can love them better, we'd best be appreciative of the opportunity to improve—not offended that we've been "doing it wrong."

When Harison was about ten years old and I asked him, "How do you know Mommy loves you?" he answered with a big grin, "When you sit with me while I play on the computer." I remember thinking, as my shoulders dropped, "What? Watch you play on the computer! You're kidding, right? What's your top five? I'll see if there's something in there that *I* enjoy."

Now, of course I didn't *say* that to him. And I became far more conscious of sitting with him and watching him play his electronic games, which he loved. I did find it interesting, though I was slightly annoyed at first that it wasn't something *I* wanted to do. That's when it hit me. Most of us are more than happy to give people what they want, as long as it fits our criteria for what we want to give! As I just said, that one-sentence formula sounds simple in theory, but I hope by now you're starting to see that in practice it may not be as easy as it sounds. It can be very tempting to give only what we want to give. If we *truly* value the relationship, however, we will willingly give the other what that person wants (without compromising our own values and beliefs, of course), but sometimes our ego or our need for control can stop us.

Once, just after I had discussed this concept in my presentation at a conference, a woman approached me. Her face lit up as she told me she was getting married in four months, but her smile faded when she mentioned, "I love receiving flowers, but my fiancé will never buy me any."

"Why not?"

"He said he doesn't *do* flowers."

"Well! Why don't you tell him that 'the shop is shut!' and it's not opening for business until we see some petals sitting in a vase! It's called consequence, baby!"

We both laughed. Then in a serious tone I added, "You're not even married yet, and if he isn't willing to buy you a lousy bunch of flowers every now and then to put a smile on your face, what else won't he be willing to do to make you happy *after* you're married?"

I don't know whether she was angry or saddened, but there on her face I could see that my words rang true. I'm so surprised and saddened when I hear of people who are not willing to do what it takes to make their partners feel happy and loved. What is that about? This is not a male/female thing either. This is simply caring enough about your partner or loved ones to bring them happiness. We can get so stuck in our need for control: "You will get what I want you to have."

Familiarity in a relationship can be like throwing water on the fire. We stop doing the magical things that we used to do for each other. We don't bother anymore with surprise gifts, a lingering kiss before leaving for work, cooking favorite meals, thinking up surprises, and so forth. There are the familiar long-running jibes from men complaining about insufficient sex in their relationships. And women complain about the lack of romance. Before marriage it was all about chocolates, dinners, walks along the beach, and whispered sweet nothings. After marriage: "Hey, babe, are you awake?" Maybe if we kept giving what we did in the beginning of our relationships, we would keep some of that magic alive.

There are endless opportunities to demonstrate our feelings for those we love. But the danger lies in trying to be a mind reader. We assume we know what they want, only to find the other person not being responsive to our "thoughtfulness." If we just ask the question and *really* listen, with empathy, we might be surprised by the other person's answer. Most of the time, the things that make people feel loved are not hard to give. For example:

I feel loved when you empty the dishwasher.

I feel loved when you take me for a meal so we can sit and talk.

I feel loved when you pick some flowers for me.

I feel loved when you give me a surprise massage.

I feel loved when you make dinner.

I feel loved when you help me in the garden.

When I say I need time to think, I feel loved when you let me be alone.

I feel loved when you help me with my homework.

I feel loved when you surprise me at work and drive me home.

I feel loved when we snuggle on the couch and watch movies.

I feel loved when you send me an "I love you" message.

I feel loved when you brush my hair.

I feel loved when we have a picnic at the beach.

I feel loved when you want to get to know my friends.

I feel loved when you tell me I look gorgeous even though you've seen this same face for twenty years.

I feel loved when you watch me play on my computer.

I feel loved when you say, "I love you."

I feel loved when you still laugh at my jokes even though you've heard them a thousand times before.

I feel loved when you're willing to do whatever it takes to make me happy.

A gentleman from an audience e-mailed me a story about asking his four-year-old son, "How do you know Daddy loves you?" He said his son stood up tall, puffed his little chest out, and said with all the pride he could muster, "When you put me in the rubber duckie, Daddy!" The father explained that he was a lifeguard at the beach, and the rubber duckie was a watercraft used to rescue people. He said he almost fell over at his son's answer, as the only reason he put him into the rubber duckie was to keep him out of harm's way! He had no idea it meant so much to his son, but his son knew it was an important vessel, so "Daddy must love me if he puts me in it!"

Don't hesitate to ask those you love, "How do you know I love you?" You, too, may be very surprised at some of the answers you get.

Remember, just find out what the other person wants— and give it to them.

Cup Filling

It astonishes me how difficult it is for some of us to say something positive to another human being—unconditionally. So often we *think* wonderful things about others and then keep the thoughts to ourselves instead of sharing them with that particular person. Here's an exercise for you: List ten positive traits that you love about your partner, parent, child, or work buddy—someone you really care about. Remember, no buts or howevers! Write down those ten things about them—and then surprise them.

For many years, I have spoken about our "emotional

muscles." We all have emotional muscles, just as we have physical muscles. I call this the "emotional muscle factor." When exercised appropriately, our emotional muscle factor gives us amazing support when dealing with the challenges of everyday life. One of the most important emotional muscles we can develop is the ability to give people the kind of feedback that helps them feel better about themselves. I call this "cup filling." We are cup filling when we fill somebody's emotional cup with comments and actions that build their self-esteem and self-belief.

Once, on a plane, I had the pleasure of being served by one of the happiest crews I had seen in a long time. I was sufficiently impressed that I wanted to say something complimentary as I was exiting the plane. Suddenly, Pitman jumped into my head and said, "Don't be silly. Don't say anything. They'll think you're stupid."

Luckily, Flipman overruled him, yelling, "Walk your talk, girl!" So as I left the plane, I placed my hand on the arm of one of the flight attendants, smiled, and said, "This is the happiest crew I have flown with in a long while. Thank you so much."

She broke into laughter, gave me a huge thank-you, and said, "You have no idea how much I needed to hear that!"

Cup filler, not cup driller.

Her reaction was enough to show me that we *all* need our cup filled occasionally.

I always have a silent chuckle when I give a compliment and the person says, "Pardon? What did you say?" so I repeat what I said. When our cup is empty, I think we like to hear compliments a couple of times!

Check to see how readily you cup fill. Do you find it easier to fill a stranger's cup than the cup of those you love? If so, is that because you have allowed yourself to become overly critical of those you love? Have you stopped looking for the wonder in what others do because you focus only on the negatives? It can be so easy to miss the magic of the intention because we get so caught up in finding fault with the person.

Is There a "But" in Your Life?

In longer-term relationships, we tend to generalize the positives and specify the negatives. We say, "I love you, but . . ." then go on to list all the things that annoy us about that person. In this way, we become "cup drillers," and we weaken the very fabric that is needed for a strong relationship.

How often do we give (or get) a cup fill only to end it with a cup drill? We make all of these great self-esteem-boosting comments and then completely destroy the effect of it by adding negative comments. We don't allow the person to digest the positives. "You're doing so well at school, *but* if you spent less time on the PlayStation or Xbox, you would do even better!" I am not saying that we don't have areas we need to work on — of course we do. We just need to make sure that we *don't pollute the positives with negatives.*

Sometimes it's wonderful to bathe in the positives for a little while. It can also make it easier to take on board the "needs improvement" comments that come our way.

Considering the impact that critical feedback can have on us, it makes sense to ensure that we counteract this with at least four to five times the amount of *positive* communication. If a person's cup is full, it probably won't be as difficult for that person to take criticism, because the positive forms a healthy buffer. On the other hand, if a person's cup is empty, he or she is not going to be as receptive to constructive feedback. In fact, it will probably sting like crazy.

Once, when a group of procrastinators attended one of my management programs, I gave them a task for homework: "When you get home tonight, do one thing you've been putting off."

On our way home in the car, I mentioned to my then-husband Rick that I was going to cook him his favorite meal, something I had been putting off for a while.

"I'm making you spaghetti Bolognese tonight, honey!" I said, so proudly, knowing just how much he adored it.

He paused for a moment, and then: "Uh, honey, it's not 'Bo-LOG-naise'! It's 'bo-lon-yaise'—the G is silent!"

"Really!" I exclaimed. "And is that like Rick with a silent P?"

It was OK—he laughed, and then so did I—but this illustrates my point: sometimes *we miss the magic in the intention, because we are too busy looking for fault in the person.*

Just like any other skill, making positive, uplifting comments takes some practice. It takes practice to notice the good in others, and it takes practice to verbalize these observations.

Pass the Compliment

When the kids were younger, we loved to play a game called Pass the Compliment. We would sit in a circle, and one of us would begin by giving the person on the right two positive comments about why he or she loved that person. The person who had received the compliments could respond only with "thank you"; then that person would *pass it on* by giving the person on his or her right two positives—and so we would work our way around our sacred hoop. We then went back the other way so that all together we gave and received different compliments to and from each other.

This was also a great game when traveling in the car, because the trip gave us time to digest the compliment, and it made us think about why we love each other and why we are loved in return.

This simple game helped my boys develop their emotional muscle factor. Each time we practice complimenting others, whether verbally or written, our emotional muscles grow. It's so rewarding to know that your words have filled another person's cup and theirs have filled yours.

Many years ago, during a presentation to an audience of over six hundred men, I suggested that they write a love letter to their children for Christmas. I went on to share a story about a male friend of mine who had never heard his father say "I love you" and how he had longed for this all his life. During the break, a gentleman came up to me and said, with tears in his eyes and a huge grin on his face, "I just sent my son a text telling him that I loved him. He sent me this back." He handed me his phone, and I saw his son's reply: "Ditto! That was rather random, Dad!" We both burst out laughing, and I could tell that his laugh was extra boisterous; as much as his son had probably loved hearing those three magical words, I think this beautiful dad had loved it too! I am sure that text will be saved forever.

Be a cup filler—not a cup driller—and see the results, right there on the faces and in the hearts of those you have touched!

Love Letters

We have so many opportunities to cup fill, but sometimes life gets in the way. I'm sorry to admit that as a parent I've spent a lot of time nagging. "Put your shoes away. Feed the dog. Clean your teeth. Set the table. Do your homework." I'm sure every parent can relate to this on some level! We can spend much of our communication time being unconsciously negative, which of course impinges on the time that might have been spent creating happy, loving memories for those whom we treasure.

What is it about the special people in your life that makes them so lovable? It's important to remind the people we love of why we love them. To help restore the balance, I write love letters. For example, every so often, I'll write a love letter to my two beautiful boys. I take some time to tell them on paper what I think is wonderful, magnificent, precious, special, unique, and fabulous about them.

An important rule when writing love letters is to never ever use the words "but" or "however" or mention anything that you're not happy with or that you feel that they could improve—otherwise, all we're doing is pouring it in at the top and drilling it out at the bottom. Think about what you can do to remind the people in your life of what you love about them. How can you fill their cup? Parents, write your sons and daughters that letter you have been putting off—for years—writing and sending! We let stupid insecurities get in the way of helping others feel fantastic. Do you really think your baby (regardless of age) is going to be correcting your grammar or punctuation? Your child will probably be trying so hard to read through misty eyes that he or she wouldn't care if it were written on toilet paper! I remember one father who was more concerned about his handwriting being messy than he was about filling his own son's cup to the brim.

My kids have kept every love letter I have given them, and I have kept theirs. I have also kept the hundreds of cards and letters that I have received from people I have presented to over the years. Whenever I feel down or need to remind myself that I do have value, I just read a bunch of these priceless gifts, and within a very short space of time, I'm feeling great again.

Whether it's a sticky note with a short message popped into a lunchbox; an e-mail from the office to tell your daughter you were thinking of how much you love her; a funny card for your lover to say that after all these years, he or she still makes your heart beat faster; a quick text to say "I love you, son"; or a five-page essay detailing every scrumptious part of them that you love—do it!

Just Do It!

I know flexing your emotional muscle factor may be hard
at first, but it's like exercising any muscle that hasn't been
given a regular workout. We may experience slight awk-
wardness at first, and the judger in us (Pitman) will be criticizing every word. But the more we work at it, the easier
it becomes, to the point where we just can't imagine life
without writing letters that make other people feel great!
We never know—it could be *our* letter that reminds them of
how special they are at a moment when they've been thinking about doing something harmful to themselves.

My mother and I had been close for many years. Unfortunately, through misconceptions, unrealistic expectations, and not seeking the truth about each other, we
drifted apart to the point that hostility became part of
our scarce communication. The climax came one night
when my mother and I had a massive phone fight about
the fallout from my marriage separation. There was a lot of
screaming and yelling (more on my part) and lots of tears
(from both of us). It was a huge showdown. Everything I
had never dared to say to her about my past came up, as
well as all the things that I had wanted from her but could
never ask for. It all came pouring out of my mouth with
venom, anger, and desperation.

I so badly wanted her to understand all that I had gone
through. I wanted her to *feel my pain and make it better.* For
many years I had tried to convince myself that I didn't need
my mother and that we weren't meant to have a close relationship. Now—feeling incredibly vulnerable—I wanted
her to be my mommy, and I wanted to be her little girl again.

But that night, something shifted. As she remained silent, I realized (later) that she was simply digesting the massive reality of my past that I had just sprung on her. She had no idea what I had gone through, because I had kept it from her so as not to hurt her. How ironic — by my wanting to *not* burden her with my truth, we ended up hurting each other anyway! When we conceal something from others, their intuition picks it up but can't decipher exactly what it is; they just know instinctively that something isn't quite right. People are not mind readers, and when we conceal our truth from them, they have to make sense of the limited information we offer. Their intuition may be screaming at them to pay attention, but we haven't given them enough information to validate their feelings.

That night, all the pieces came together for my mother and me. Now, we didn't magically create a new bond overnight. It took lots of time, lots of talking, and lots of patience and acceptance.

A few months after this eventful night, I took a short trip to New Zealand, and my mother babysat my boys. As I was leaving, I noticed a handwritten letter from my mother. I started to read. I tried to fight back the tears. My breath was taken away. My mother had written me a love letter! Not just any old love letter. It was the most beautiful love letter in the world. She had written it for me, and in that moment, as I blinked tears onto the page, I felt totally connected to her.

I felt her love, and I knew she understood my past, which she knew she couldn't change. Just knowing she was there for me, proud of me and loving me, was everything I needed. That letter is now safely laminated, and every time

I read it, I am reminded of my mother's love.

As I sat in Auckland Airport waiting, pen in hand, for my flight home, the words just flowed onto the page as I wrote a love letter back to her. To think we had missed out on ten years because we'd lost our way! She's in her eighties now, and I'm so grateful we've found our way back to each other. Some people say they don't have regrets. Well, I do. I regret that I lost those ten years because of ignorance, pride, and misunderstanding. I have learned the heavy price of not standing in my truth, and the damage that secrets can do to a relationship. I realized too late that my arrogant need to be right had stopped me from having those tough conversations earlier. *The only way out is through* — I had tried to avoid the pain of confrontation by pretending I didn't care. And all I have is *now* — so I am going to not waste another minute.

Love letters work. I will keep writing those letters to my family and friends, and I hope you will write yours too.

I luf Mum yes.
—Jackson, age five

I've learned that people will forget what you said, people will forget what you did, but people will never forget how you made them feel.

— MAYA ANGELOU

Chapter 17

The Buck Stops Here

Why wait to be great? It's either NOW or TOO LATE! The only time we have is this moment right now, and it's up to us what we do with it. The moment you had five minutes ago is gone forever! That's how life works. How we act in each moment is up to us. Giving 100 percent means giving it everything we have. It's about playing at 100 percent in all that we do—whether it's kicking a ball with our kids, working on a business document, riding a bike in the park, or having an afternoon nap. It's about doing it all to the best of our ability and being in the moment. It's also about being passionate.

My father taught me about passion and giving 100 percent when I landed my first job at age fifteen, scrubbing cupboards in a cafeteria. Not my idea of a great vocation!

Dad was dying of cancer at the time, and one day, before I left home to catch the bus for my first day at work, he called me into his bedroom. Lying in bed, he said, "Go scrub those cupboards, girl, like there's no tomorrow."

"But Dad," I whined, "I don't want a job scrubbing greasy cupboards!"

"It's good money, so go and do the job," he said. We were struggling financially as a family, and the money would be very welcome.

After our conversation, I remember travelling on the bus at 4:30 a.m. with a completely different perception. I was no longer scrubbing cupboards; I was saving my family! I scrubbed those cupboards so hard I almost brought the wood grain to the surface again! I finished the day with greasy hair, greasy skin, and my boss admiring my hard work. Well, let me tell you—within three weeks, I was the milkshake maker. Straight up that corporate ladder!

What my dad was really telling me was the old quote from Voltaire that Stephen R. Covey has made famous: "The enemy of the 'best' is often the 'good.'"

When I heard those words, my first reaction was "Huh?" I had to play that message over and over in my head until it clicked with me. The enemy of your *best* is when you choose *good* instead.

How are the kids doing? Good.

How's work? Good.

How's that school project? Good.

How's life been? Good.

How was the holiday? Good.

It's as if we accept "good" as our standard—not our best! Imagine what might happen if we aimed for our best instead of good, every time. We could quite possibly have the most wonderful life imaginable! But why don't we? We get too comfortable doing what we know, aiming for goals we're certain can be easily achieved. We do them at a level that no longer presents a challenge for us, one that avoids the possibility of stress. Especially as we get older, we tend to shrink our fear zone and stretch our comfort zone; not wanting to be challenged, we settle for easy and then wonder why the *joie de vivre* has gone from our life. Good enough becomes our standard, and we make excuses for why we can't give our best.

I invite you: the next time you're walking along the beach or at the park or even just sitting at the dinner table with the people or person you have chosen to spend your life with, really be there as if you will never ever be with them in that place again. Reach deep inside yourself and find what you need to say or do to support those you love. We all tend to complain about our lives, but what if we considered the alternatives? What if we didn't have what we have? I can't imagine my life without my two boys. Nothing in our lives together is ever so bad that I would ever want to change that. When we consider the alternatives, I think we realize just how fortunate we really are.

The next time you're holding a baby in your arms, hold that baby like you'll never hold another baby again. It may seem a strange thing to say, especially if you don't have children, but I'm suggesting you hold that baby tenderly for the memory of a fourteen-month-old son of an old friend. Morgan was only fourteen months old when his little life ended. I used to bounce my babies in my arms to help them fall asleep (I think there's something special about falling asleep in your mother's arms). Some nights, my arms would hurt from their weight, so I would just bounce them faster! I would get really frustrated, feel angry, and think, "Just go to sleep, will you?" But then I thought of beautiful Morgan and said to myself with gratitude, "Hurt away, it doesn't matter; I have my baby in my arms."

The same applies to your work. The next time you're serving someone in your role—whether in business, as a volunteer, or in community service, serve that human being as if you'll never, ever be able to serve him or her again. Serve that person as if tonight she or he will die, and you're one of the last people to make a powerful, positive impact on that person's life. When you hold people in such a special, vulnerable place, you really do reach deep inside and pull out the best "you" that you have to offer. Remember, this is someone's Book of Life, and every action, every deed, and every thought makes an imprint somewhere.

We spend so much time focusing on ourselves that we forget how powerful we can be in the life of another. Lao Tzu, author of the *Tao Te Ching*, explained, "There is no more noble job on earth than to be of service to another human being!" We all have an ability to sense what is real and what isn't. If we pay enough attention, these truths will come to us from anywhere and anyone.

The Truth

Perhaps something stirred in you as you read this book. I hope you paid attention. Sometimes it can be hard for us to hear the truth within because we may be so stuck in a certain behavior that we're not yet willing to let go of it and move on. I know some people who keep themselves sick (unconsciously, but also sometimes consciously) because of the benefits they get from being sick. Those benefits may be attention, being excused from responsibilities they'd rather avoid, less pressure, or even dependency—whatever benefit or secondary gain they get overrides the freedom of living their life in truth. "It's not my fault!" they cry, as they continue to refrain from doing anything that will contribute to their getting better.

It's just the same when we blame others for the way we react. Our anger, sarcasm, aloofness, and self-pity all become someone else's fault. "If they hadn't behaved that way, I wouldn't have reacted this way!" is the cry of the person who denies the truth of her own lack of self-control.

Our Pitman will tempt us to run from truth at times, and it can be overwhelming to take total personal responsibility for ourselves, but at the end of the day, only our truth, along with the courage of our Flipman, will set us on the right path.

Being honest is simply telling your own truth—your truth as it is for you, within you. Not what you've been taught to believe, not what you've read, but the deep, inner knowing that tells you the difference between right and wrong, good and bad. We each have our own internal compass, our own Flipman that will always guide us to that honest place, if we pay attention. I'm not talking about not stealing $200 out of the till, or not taking a few cookies from the cookie jar. It's not that sort of honesty. The honesty and truth I'm talking about is our personal honesty. We, and our internal Flipman, are the judge and jury of our personal honesty. We don't have anyone outside of us who can really determine whether we're being honest or not.

I remember someone commenting on another's authen-
ticity. The only person who truly knows whether you are
authentic or not is you. The truth that has the greatest
impact on your life is your own personal truth. "The truth
will set you free." That is such a powerful biblical statement. The truth really will set you free.

I know a woman who held a secret about her past for
almost her entire life because she had labeled it as shame-
ful. This experience happened *to* her, yet in some way, as
many of us do, she blamed herself. When she "came out"
about her experiences to those she loved, years and years
of anguish and torment were washed away in moments,
because everything made sense. The way she mothered her
children, the way she allowed people to treat her, the way
she held bitter attitudes that didn't seem to be congruent
with who she was, the way she emotionally distanced herself from those she loved. When she shared the secrets of
her past, she created meaning for her behaviors and attitudes, and everyone understood why she was the way she
was. Her truth set everyone free!

We all have a story, and I have a huge amount of compassion for events that people have experienced. I also
know that when we use these stories as excuses, we are not
living in truth; we are living in the Pit.

Claim Ownership of Your Story and Your Life

Honesty is about taking ownership and responsibility. If
we're going to change our world, then we had better start
changing ourselves first. As we now know, when we're in
the Pit it's so easy to place issues outside of ourselves. If

our relationship ends acrimoniously, it can be tempting to lay blame on the other side, especially when we're filled with bitterness and the need for revenge. Pitman loves it when we're being the victim. "You did this to me; you caused me all this pain; you ruined my life!" It is no one else's job to make you feel happy, satisfied, or loved. It's *your* responsibility. Claiming ownership of your story and taking personal responsibility means that you're in charge of your life.

I've seen people waste an entire lifetime holding on to bitterness. The Irish-American actor, writer, and politician Malachy McCourt said, "Resentment is like taking poison and waiting for the other person to die." Being bitter eats at you and gets in the way of your living a full and joyful Flipman life. Allowing ourselves to hate is self-indulgent and self-destructive, and it also preoccupies us so we don't have to focus on owning our part or creating the life that will really serve us well. There are always two sides to a story, and the more in denial we are about our part in the movie, the more elaborate we get with the script writing. We have a choice: we can easily exaggerate our story, or we can sit in our *truth* and just own our part. Bring it in. Even if that means simply learning to forgive, then so be it. Forgiving yourself or someone else, though not easy, can transform your life. I'm not saying this in a lighthearted way at all; I know from personal experience that some circumstances take a lot of healing. But this is your life, and when you stay bitter and stuck in your past, you give your life away.

On the other hand, when we look at our issues like an explorer, we can start to search for familiar patterns. Relationships in particular offer us the opportunity to observe some of our most appropriate and inappropriate behaviors, beliefs, and values. No one is completely innocent in the complexities of a relationship, and in most cases it takes two to make it work or not work. It takes courage to accept and own our truth, but when we do, the path is cleared for incredible growth. So listen. Pay attention in those moments when it hurts to hear the truth. Be dissociated and see the situation as an observer watching your movie. Ask, "What do I need to learn from this? What am I supposed to be getting here?" Flipman will help you find an answer. It may not happen immediately, and it may not be easy, but if you're serious about getting your truth, then you will find it, because the truth will set you free.

If you need to, create a new story. Create a new vision for your life, using these wonderful experiences as great teachers that have resulted in a wiser and more powerful you. You are not broken, you don't need fixing, and you are not dysfunctional. Everything that has happened to you has been part of the great mystery called *you*! Each event, each heartbreak, and each triumph guides you step-by-step to your *true* self. All of your life's experiences have been part of the formula to create the *you* that is here *now*.

Commitment

One of the most common traits of successful people is commitment. Commitment is being willing to do whatever it takes to get the job done—regardless! It could be mowing the lawn, going to your child's concert, running a company with integrity, being honest, or being fit and healthy. It doesn't really matter what the goal is; we can achieve it as long as we have commitment. Commitment in a relationship is often a funny thing. Most of us would say that we're committed to our partner and kids, to our employer or staff, to our friends. But when things get a bit tough, most people in a relationship will threaten each other with ending the relationship:

"Go on then, pack your bags. I'm not stopping you."

"I've had it with this relationship; I'm out of here!"

"They wouldn't know what hit them if I left this place!"

We may say these things in jest, but remember that the unconscious mind believes everything we say.

As Harville Hendricks explains in his wonderful relationship book, *Getting the Love You Want*, when we make comments like that, we put "chinks in our relationship armor." No wonder so many of us are walking around feeling battered!

People wonder why the magic leaves their relationship, yet if they were really committed to it, they would listen to the dialogue they use when communicating with their partner. Sarcasm, nasty little jibes, criticism, and judgment all serve to decay the very foundation we've been trying to build. Be a cup filler and write those love letters. Do what you can to find your way back to each other.

Why WAIT to be GREAT?
It's either NOW or TOO LATE!

It's time for you and me to say goodbye for now and start living our *Flipman* life. I hope you've come to realize that all of us are on this journey together, and we all have our struggles and our triumphs. Success is not about avoiding the challenging experiences of life; it's about embracing them, really *feeling* them, and becoming a better person as a result.

Here are my final thoughts for you:

- Change the way you view your past events. Our life lessons are encased in those events, just waiting for us to discover them.

- Use Flipman as your support mechanism, always being aware of the seductiveness of Pitman. Flipman's Strategy — See it! Say it! Feel it! Do it! — is the key to creating desired change.

- You are writing in the Book of Life. Write something wonderful and positive in yours and in the books of those you love. Be a cup filler, not a cup driller!

- Fear is just a heartbeat. Breathe through it and learn to manage it!

- Have the courage to be the explorer in your own life. Find your greatness and know that your place in life is a vital one. If you don't know your life's purpose, relax; you're probably doing it anyway!

- Never fear the truth. Take responsibility for your life and embrace whatever it offers. Life is so precious, and each and every one of us has many gifts. For some of us, these gifts have been buried in the heaviness and darkness of the Pit, but they are there. *Never, ever stop looking.*

► And last, let's not avoid our pain anymore. Instead, embrace it, accept it, thank it, and be grateful for it. This book is not about replaying our painful stories every chance we get to whoever will listen. It's about walking into our pain, staring our past right in the face, and reclaiming our power. This is when we transform our experience into wisdom.

How can we learn compassion and sensitivity for our fellow man without being hurt or moved by our own life experiences? Remember the difference between sympathy and empathy. Taking responsibility for yourself comes first, because when you take responsibility for yourself, you're in a much better state to help others — to be of service to other human beings, without harboring bitterness and revenge.

To serve another with love in your heart — that, to me, is the greatest joy on earth, the greatest gift you can give.

All my love,

Terry
xxx o x

Acknowledgments

This book would still be in my head, my heart, and my frustrations were it not for the countless Flipmen I have encountered on my journey. To you, I say the biggest thank-you imaginable! Thank you for trusting me, thank you for your courage in letting Flipman rule, and thank you for sharing a few words in our Book of Life together. To my own internal Flipman, thank you for giving me the power of choice. In every moment, I realize that it is my perception and my consequential actions that create my pain or joy, and through you I am able to connect with my inner spirit.

To my two beautiful sons, Harison and Jackson: how can I ever thank you for all that you give to this world and to me? Your courage, your insights, and your complete honesty are a constant reminder to me of why all of this matters. You have touched my heart and my soul like no other and have given me the greatest name of my life—Mum!

I have also had the great fortune of being exposed to some of the finest teachers, educators, and guides on the planet. Whether the learning came through a personal connection, a program I attended, a book that I read, or a conversation, my life has been transformed because of all the lives that have crossed my path.

And finally, to my beautiful mother! Mum, you have been through so much and have led such an incredible life. I feel blessed that it was your face looking at me when I was born; you have left your footprints on my heart forever. I thank you for having the courage to revisit your past, understand it, and face your own journey of self-discovery, regardless of the pain it roused in you. You are such an inspiration, and I love you with all my soul.

Index

abuse
    grief and, 52, 59–60
    meaning of, 49, 54–58
    service and, 58–59
addiction, 39, 125, 143. *See also*
    alcohol; smoking
affirmations, 99
alcohol, 121–127
Allen, Woody, 60
Angelou, Maya, 168
Aurelius, Marcus, 82
blame
    feedback and, 70–71
    language of, 77–78
    pain and, 142–143
    pit and, 40, 77, 117, 175
    responsibility and, 73–76,
        80–81, 173

body
    abuse and, 56
    grief and, 38
    language, 14–15
    pain and, 137
    perception and, 92, 94–96,
        100, 104, 106, 112
Book of Life, 147–152, 172
brain, 45, 107–109. *See also*
    neurons
Brand, Carl, 82

change. *See* transition
choice
    Flipman as, 9, 97, 104, 130–132
    good as, 170
    habits and, 121–123, 125–126
    happiness as, 73–81
    responsibility for, 134, 140
commitment, 176–177. *See also*
    ownership; responsibility
courage, 25, 50–51, 178. *See also*
    fear
Covey, Stephen R., 170
cup filling, 159–161, 164–165, 177

depression, sleeping and, 128–129
dissociation, 47–49, 52–53, 83

emotions
    allowing, 15–16
    avoiding, 3, 42
    changing, 51
    conquering, 143–146
    expressing, 38–39, 142
    healthy, 13, 38–40, 76
    perception and, 95
    reactive, 13, 38, 64–65
    See also pain
empathy
    abuse and, 55
    assumptions and, 33–34
    conflict and, 152
    defined, 28–29

Other Products by Terry Hawkins

Books:

Why Wait to Be Great? It's Either Now *or* Too Late!

Secrets of Inspiring Women EXPOSED (contributor)

Make Your Fortune by 40 (contributor)

The Power of More Than One (contributor)

20/20 A Fresh Look at Business Growth (contributor)

The Power of Good: True Stories of Great Kindness (contributor)

Coaching Programs:

Terry has also authored a series of CD and DVD coaching programs, including comprehensive workbooks.

S.E.L.L.

L.E.A.D.

NOW & TOO LATE!

CREATE your LIFE!

FITNESS 5 FACTOR

Subscriptions:

Terry also delivers a monthly forty-five-minute CD and flash card, *Talking with Terry* (*TWT*), to her subscription base around the world.

Free "Pit of Misery" and "Flipman's Strategy" cartoons can be downloaded at:

www.TerryHawkins.com/WWTBGdownloads

For more information or to purchase products, please visit www.TerryHawkins.com.

About the Author

Terry Hawkins grew up in a large family in suburban Brisbane, Queensland, Australia. After a challenging childhood and teenage years, Terry became driven to achieve in her career. Her early promotion to the position of training coordinator for a major fashion retailer unleashed a love for helping people achieve their potential. After much success as an employee, Terry took the plunge at the age of twenty-seven and opened her enterprise training company, People In Progress. In 1989, with $167, a card table, and an old computer held together with a rubber band, Terry established her training company People In Progress Global (now with offices in Australia and the U.S.). Terry quickly gained a reputation as a talented and results-achieving business educator, assisting companies in their sales, service, and leadership transformations.

Her passion for understanding people and their behaviors, and her ability to simplify the most complex theories made her a favorite both as a trainer and as a highly sought-after keynote speaker, speaking on performance, overcoming obstacles, and strategies for sustained change.

Terry's career as an author began in 2006 when she published her first book, *NOW & TOO LATE!* in response to constant requests from her audiences. She followed this with her children's series, which offers sage advice for children in the challenging areas of obesity, divorce, difference and racism, and disabilities and cancer. *Why Wait to Be Great? It's Either Now or Too Late!* is the newest addition to the collection.

When not on the road, Terry lives in Los Angeles with her two teenage sons, Harison and Jackson. While Terry expands her Australian training operation, People In Progress Global, into the United States, she also continues her successful speaking career. She is a Certified Master Practitioner of NLP, Time Line Therapy, and hypnotherapy and holds the Certified Speaking Professional (CSP) level with the National Speakers Association, an accreditation held by only about 10 percent of speakers worldwide. Having won numerous business, speaking, and service awards, Terry continues her quest to make a powerful, positive impact on the human condition.

For more information on People In Progress, visit: www.PeopleInProgressGlobal.com

Berrett–Koehler
Publishers

Berrett-Koehler is an independent publisher dedicated to an ambitious mission: *Creating a World That Works for All*.

We believe that to truly create a better world, action is needed at all levels—individual, organizational, and societal. At the individual level, our publications help people align their lives with their values and with their aspirations for a better world. At the organizational level, our publications promote progressive leadership and management practices, socially responsible approaches to business, and humane and effective organizations. At the societal level, our publications advance social and economic justice, shared prosperity, sustainability, and new solutions to national and global issues.

A major theme of our publications is "Opening Up New Space." Berrett-Koehler titles challenge conventional thinking, introduce new ideas, and foster positive change. Their common quest is changing the underlying beliefs, mindsets, institutions, and structures that keep generating the same cycles of problems, no matter who our leaders are or what improvement programs we adopt.

We strive to practice what we preach—to operate our publishing company in line with the ideas in our books. At the core of our approach is stewardship, which we define as a deep sense of responsibility to administer the company for the benefit of all of our "stakeholder" groups: authors, customers, employees, investors, service providers, and the communities and environment around us.

We are grateful to the thousands of readers, authors, and other friends of the company who consider themselves to be part of the "BK Community." We hope that you, too, will join us in our mission.

A BK Life Book

This book is part of our BK Life series. BK Life books change people's lives. They help individuals improve their lives in ways that are beneficial for the families, organizations, communities, nations, and world in which they live and work. To find out more, visit **www.bk-life.com**.

Berrett–Koehler
Publishers

A community dedicated to creating
a world that works for all

Visit Our Website: www.bkconnection.com

Read book excerpts, see author videos and Internet movies, read
our authors' blogs, join discussion groups, download book apps, find
out about the BK Affiliate Network, browse subject-area libraries of
books, get special discounts, and more!

Subscribe to Our Free E-Newsletter, the *BK Communiqué*

Be the first to hear about new publications, special discount offers,
exclusive articles, news about bestsellers, and more! Get on the list
for our free e-newsletter by going to **www.bkconnection.com**.

Get Quantity Discounts

Berrett-Koehler books are available at quantity discounts for orders
of ten or more copies. Please call us toll-free at (800) 929-2929 or
email us at bkp.orders@aidcvt.com.

Join the BK Community

BKcommunity.com is a virtual meeting place where people from
around the world can engage with kindred spirits to create a world
that works for all. BKcommunity.com members may create their own
profiles, blog, start and participate in forums and discussion groups,
post photos and videos, answer surveys, announce and register for
upcoming events, and chat with others online in real time. Please join
the conversation!

Certified

Corporation
bcorporation.net